CONTENTS

A PEOPLE READY FOR THE RETURN OF JESUS

Adventist Laymen's League
Crusade for Christ Bible Study Guides

VOLUME 2

by Emilio B. Knechtle
and Charles J. Sohlmann

PACIFIC PRESS PUBLISHING ASSOCIATION
Mountain View, California
Omaha, Nebraska   Oshawa, Ontario

"Christ in You, the Hope of Glory"

INTRODUCTION

God created man for Himself. In a spiritual sense, He desires to have an intimate love relationship with us and share with us the joy and happiness of life.

Through the institution of marriage God gave us a symbol of the intimate union He desires to have with us.

For a time God's wonderful plans for us were frustrated by the rebellion of Satan and by the unfaithfulness of man.

Despite these tragic events God did not forsake His long-range plan for mankind. He was willing to take drastic steps in order to prevent the alienation of man from Him. He loved us more than His own life. "In all their affliction He was afflicted . . . : in His love and in His pity He redeemed them." Isaiah 63:9. Christ, our Creator, was willing to become the Son of man and take the curse of our rebellion upon Himself. This meant His own death. Thus He reconciled a stubborn and antagonistic humanity with the Godhead. He bridged the infinite gulf between God and man by conquering sin and death through the cross.

Through the incarnation, life, death, and resurrection of Christ, we are brought nearer to God than if we had never sinned. God the Father gave His Son forever to mankind. Christ will always remain the Son of man and retain His ties with humanity throughout eternity.

Someday in the future the terrible era of sin and death will terminate and sin and sinners will be no more. Then the whole universe will be composed of beings who live together in unselfish love and harmony. In that new world God the Father, Jesus Christ, and the Holy Spirit will share a blissful life with the redeemed. God will dwell forever with His family which He bought back with the blood of His own Son. The righteous will see God face to face. The apostle John gives a wonderful insight into the new world in the book of Revelation. He points to the fact that God's original purpose will finally be accomplished despite the long delay. The new earth will be populated with the believers of the Old and New Testament eras. The history of this world will be to them like a bad dream that is past. When we are finally united with God on the new earth, nothing will ever again separate us from Him. There will never be another rebellion.

Jesus Christ was not satisfied to wait until His return before having an intimate love relationship with the believer. He did not wish to wait until the end of earth's history before effecting this union with man. In His infinite love Jesus Christ designed a plan which makes it possible for us to enter into this wonderful relationship with Him even now. John 6:56.

Christ made a way to the hearts of fallen men; He enabled them to break away from the power of Satan and the dominion of sin and to become united with Him through the Holy Spirit. You can be one with Jesus Christ although you are still living in a fallen world that is ruled by the prince of darkness.

I. "WE WOULD LIKE TO SEE JESUS"

A. Christ is the secret desire of every human heart.

When Christ was on earth, a number of Greeks desired to see Him. They were believers in the true God and were seeking for more knowledge of Him. They heard that Jesus was teaching in the temple and that He was regarded as the expected Messiah. They approached Philip, a disciple of Christ, with the words, "Sir, we would like to see Jesus." They waited for Him in the court of the Gentiles that was located in the Jewish temple. John 12:20, 21, NEB.

Since the beginning of time the highest aspiration of

the human heart has been to contact God; the restless heart longs for such an experience. Moses cried out, "I beseech Thee, show me Thy glory." Exodus 33:18. Job prayed, "Oh that I knew where I might find Him! that I might come even to His seat!" Job 23:3. David exclaimed, "One thing have I desired of the Lord, . . . that I may . . . behold the beauty of the Lord." Psalm 27:4.

Jesus Christ promised the redeemed the privilege of seeing God when He said, "Blessed are the pure in heart: for they shall see God." Matthew 5:8. The apostle John speaks of a face-to-face experience in Revelation 22:4, when he says, "And they shall see His face; and His name shall be in their foreheads."

B. **Christ is revealed through the lives of His followers.**

Since the ascension of Jesus Christ people all over the world have desired to see His face, have longed to love, to know, and to follow Him. There is only one way for people today to see Christ, and that is for Him to be visible in His disciples. Jesus wishes to be revealed to the world through His followers. Christians are to reflect Jesus Christ. He expressed this desire in His prayer before His death: "I in them, and Thou in Me, that they may be made perfect in one; and that the world may know that Thou hast sent Me, and hast loved them, as Thou hast loved Me." John 17:23. If only the world could see Jesus in the lives of His followers!

When Jesus lives in the human soul, the love of God radiates out of that person. The love of God has an enormous power of transformation. It changes the expression of our faces, our voices; it transforms our behavior and our thinking. The character traits of Jesus appear in our own nature. God made us originally to reflect Him, and God's plan of redemption is meant to restore the divine image in us. This is what Paul was thinking of when he said, "For whom He did foreknow, He also did predestinate to be conformed to the image of His Son." Romans 8:29.

The indwelling Christ through the Holy Spirit changes the face and character of every true believer in such a drastic way that people around him become aware of it. Acts 4:13; 2 Corinthians 3:18. The believers in the Galatian church refused this change in their lives, and Paul was constrained to appeal to them in these words, "My little children, of whom I travail in birth again until Christ be formed in you." Galatians 4:19.

We cannot wear the image of Christ on the outside like a mask. It must be an experience of the heart. It cannot be an imitation of Christ, it must be a reproduction of Christ. When the Spirit of Christ dwells in a person, his character will not change in trouble, or in trials, or in the face of obstacles, or in suffering. The power of Christ will lead him through these difficult experiences and give him the victory.

Jesus Christ does not force Himself upon the believer. When we were converted, we asked Jesus Christ to cleanse us with His blood from all our sins. In the same way the believer must ask and invite Jesus Christ to abide in him. This is our responsibility. Only then can the Holy Spirit begin to work in us. Man must cooperate with the Holy Spirit. Paul put it this way in Colossians 3:10, "Put on the new man, which is renewed in knowledge after the image of Him that created him."

II. CHRIST IN YOU IS THE HOPE OF GLORY
A. How is the miracle of transformation possible?

You may say, "I love to sin. How is it possible for me ever to hate it? I love my life. How will I ever be willing to lose it?" Man has a free will; he can refuse to allow Christ to change his character, his thoughts, his ambitions. Man can say No to God. Before God can do any act of transformation in our hearts, we must first consent to it. Multitudes of Christians are able to witness to the fact that God has completely changed their characters.

This is indeed the greatest miracle that can happen to man. No doctor, no psychologist, is in a position to transform our natures so drastically as does the indwelling Christ.

B. **Men dead in sin can experience the spiritual resurrection.**

The drastic change in the character of man by the power of God is illustrated in the Old Testament in the following story:

When the Israelites rebelled against Aaron, God directed Moses to put the rods of the leaders in front of the ark in the tabernacle. God promised that He would demonstrate through a miracle whom He had chosen to be high priest. Numbers 17:8 tells the result: "And, behold, the rod of Aaron for the house of Levi was budded, and brought forth buds, and bloomed blossoms, and yielded almonds." God is able to resurrect dead matter and make it bring forth fruit. God will do this in a spiritually dead person.

The budding rod of Aaron is a picture of a spiritual resurrection, a new birth. To be in Christ literally means to have the life of God in us. Too many Christians interpret believing to mean an intellectual assent to a set of doctrines. Christians can be orthodox and believe everything the Bible says and still lose their souls. In the parable of the ten virgins Jesus Christ spoke of five foolish virgins who believed that the bridegroom was coming, but they were not ready for him. When he came, they were rejected. These five foolish virgins stand for orthodox, Bible-believing Christians who lack the indwelling Spirit of Christ.

C. **Christ in you is the crowning evidence of conversion.**

People can attack the divine inspiration of the Bible; they can deny the existence of God; but they cannot deny the evidence that Christ lives in a person. When Jesus Christ radiates His love through the life of a surrendered Christian, people are attracted to Christ. Paul called this experience the essence of Christianity.

"The riches of the glory of this mystery among the Gentiles; which is Christ in you, the hope of glory." Colossians 1:27. At the Last Supper Jesus Christ promised this experience to His followers: "If a man love Me, he will keep My words; and My Father will love him, and We will come unto him, and make Our abode with him." John 14:23. When we give consent for the Holy Spirit to put to death our selfish nature, Jesus Christ is able to reign in our lives: "I am crucified with Christ; nevertheless I live; yet not I, but Christ liveth in me; and the life which I now live in the flesh I live by the faith of the Son of God, who loved me, and gave Himself for me." Galatians 2:20.

This miracle of re-creation is brought about by the Holy Spirit. It is awe-inspiring to think that God Himself is willing to dwell in us. Body and soul become His living temple; He transforms us into the glorious image of Jesus Christ. "We . . . beholding as in a glass the glory of the Lord, are changed into the same image from glory to glory even as by the Spirit of the Lord." 2 Corinthians 3:18. When Christ is living in a newborn soul, His influence on the behavior betrays the presence of a divine power. "For God, who commanded the light to shine out of darkness, hath shined in our hearts, to give the light of the knowledge of the glory of God in the face of Jesus Christ." 2 Corinthians 4:6.

III. INTELLECTUAL CONSENT VERSUS SPIRITUAL EXPERIENCE
A. Believing is loving Jesus Christ.

The love of the world, the love of pleasure, materialism, skepticism, false philosophies, the theory of evolution, et cetera, have defaced the image of Christ in many Christians. Often churchgoing Christians are luke-warm toward Jesus Christ. When unbelievers approach these Christians, they cannot see Jesus in them. Such Christians know the teachings of Christ, but they do not know Him personally. Many turn away from such Christians and never investigate the claims of Christ again; they are repulsed by the cold, legalistic, hard natures.

When Moses returned from Mount Sinai, his face shone. Exodus 34:35. Jesus Christ was shining out of him. When Stephen stood before the council of the Sanhedrin, they saw that his face was shining like that of an angel. Acts 6:15. It was Christ shining through Stephen. The apostle Paul spoke of a divine treasure which radiates its power through us. This treasure is Jesus Christ living in the believer. "We have this treasure in earthen vessels, to show that the transcendent power belongs to God and not to us." 2 Corinthians 4:7, RSV.

B. **Believers can easily lose this power.**

Samson was a chosen vessel, a prophet of God. He was given enormous strength, but spiritually he was bankrupt. He had chosen a sensual life and refused the power of God to give him victory. Finally he lost his physical strength, without being aware of it. Judges 16:20. This was the tragic experience of a great man of God, but it can happen to any Christian. Christ is saying to the Christians today; "Thou sayest, I am rich, and increased with goods, and have need of nothing; and knowest not that thou art wretched, and miserable, and poor, and blind, and naked." Revelation 3:17. Christians can be intellectual giants, leaders of churches, great orators, and be spiritually blind; their natures can be cold and hard. Christians can be ardent defenders of their faith, unswerving in loyalty to the Biblical doctrines, fascinated by wonderful prophecies; they can work hard, always presenting the best possible case for their faith before the world; they can believe profoundly in the triumph of truth in God's last messages, and still lose their souls.

Our faith can be an allegiance to a system of doctrinal truths, fidelity to a message from God. Our

Christianity can be primarily a devoted mental assent to a beautiful, logical, Heaven-sent framework of truth rather than a new life in Christ. Believing in Jesus is often considered as staking our lives on the credibility of certain theological tenets rather than on a love relationship with Jesus Christ. Christ should become a living reality in our lives; we should experience His transforming power at work in us.

C. **Christ is waiting to be asked to dwell in you.**

"As many as received Him, to them gave He power to become the sons of God." John 1:12. Ask Jesus to invade your heart, to live His life in you, to give you His goodness, His purity, His love for others. What the cause of Christ needs most today is Christians like Jesus, not only flaming prophets, but examples of mercy, grace, and pity. We should have but one desire, to be like Jesus. "I dwell . . . with him . . . that is of a contrite and humble spirit." Isaiah 57:15. When God and man are thus united, then man becomes partaker of the divine nature and supernatural things can happen. 2 Peter 1:3, 4.

Originally Christ created man in His own image, but we lost this divine image. The purpose of salvation is to restore this image in us, that we might "be conformed to the image of His Son." Romans 8:29.

IV. THERE IS A GREAT HUNGER IN THE HEARTS OF MEN TODAY; THEY WANT TO SEE JESUS

A. **The world desires to see Christ in us.**

As the Greeks prior to the crucifixion of Jesus came to Jerusalem and desired to see Him, so today, just prior to Christ's return, large numbers of people have a secret longing to know Jesus Christ. They are seeking the true believers, those who have a living relationship with the Lord and are faithful to His teachings, the truths once delivered to His saints. There are men and women in our age in whom Jesus is fully dwelling. Seekers after God come to them saying, "Sir, we wish to see Jesus. Please tell us what Jesus has done for you. Does He really live in you through the Holy Spirit? Show us the results in your life."

Can you say to such a person, "Yes, Jesus Christ is living in me; He has changed my life completely; He rules over my mind, heart, soul, and body; I can do all things through Him; I love Him with all my heart and mind and strength; I am happy to help you find Jesus too"? Can you honestly say this to another person? Men can see Jesus today only as He lives in His followers.

Flesh and blood cannot inherit the kingdom of God. Those who still wear the image of the earthly Adam will not be allowed to enter heaven. We must wear the image of the heavenly Adam, Jesus Christ. 1 Corinthians 15:49, 50. This divine work of transformation is presently taking place in men and women all around the world. If we do not experience it, we lose our souls. Is it happening to you? "How comest thou in hither not having a wedding garment? ... Cast him into outer darkness." Matthew 22:12, 13.

B. **We may look into eternity**.

When Jesus Christ comes to earth the second time "to be glorified in His saints, and to be admired in all them that believe" (2 Thessalonians 1:10), on whom will He bestow immortality? Whom will He take with Him to heaven? He will take all those to heaven in whose faces He is reflected, in whose lives He can be seen, whose characters are like His. Although in this life we will never cease growing spiritually, Christ will impute to us whatever righteousness is missing in us. We will become exactly as He is.

When the redeemed of God appear in heaven, the angels and sinless beings inhabiting the universe will gaze with amazement at them. As they behold the redeemed host, they will recognize in each one of them the image of Jesus Christ.

When Philip, full of unbelief, said to Jesus at the Last Supper, "Lord, show us the Father, and it sufficeth us," Jesus answered him, "Have I been so long time with you, and yet hast thou not known Me, Philip? he that hath seen Me hath seen the Father." John 14:8, 9. If people come to you saying, "Sir, we would like to see Jesus," are you certain that they will leave you with the impression that they have seen Him reflected in you? This is the demand of the hour. For that purpose we were born.

The Glorious Climax of the Plan of Redemption

INTRODUCTION

The two most important events in the history of the earth are the first and second comings of Jesus Christ. All other episodes revolve around these two points and focus men's attention on the fact that Divinity directly intervenes in human affairs. One has already occurred; now we anticipate the second.

I. THE LORD JESUS DEFINITELY PROMISED TO RETURN TO THIS EARTH AGAIN

A. Why is Christ's return delayed?

Jesus promised at the Last Supper, "I will come again." John 14:3. A great deal of time has elapsed since He ascended to heaven, and many Christians have lost their faith in His second coming, much as the Jews had lost their faith in the first appearance of the Messiah.

There is a reason behind Christ's delay. The delay is meant to test our faith. Jesus did not give us a date for His second coming. Why?

1. Many would have been discouraged by the prospect of having to wait such a long time.
2. Others would have postponed their "conversion" until the end of their lives.
3. Jesus intended that those of every generation should wait for Him as fervently as possible, and prepare for His coming as if this event would happen in their

lifetime. The only time for man to prepare himself spiritually for the coming of Jesus Christ is in his lifetime. Character cannot be changed after death.

B. **His tarrying will not last indefinitely.**

His glorious return is not to be postponed indefinitely. In the next lesson we will study significant world events predicted by Jesus and His apostles which show us the conditions that will prevail on the earth at the time of His coming. The Jewish nation did not expect the Messiah when Jesus came to this earth 2,000 years ago. It is strange that today a similar condition exists in the Christian church. The majority of Christians are repeating the same error by remaining ignorant and unprepared for the second appearing of Jesus. When we lose faith in His second coming, we also lose the joy of looking forward to that great event. We lose spiritual power and alertness which are most needed in the last battles with the forces of evil. Such Christians become like the five foolish virgins in the parable. "When the Son of Man cometh, shall He find faith on the earth?" Luke 18:8.

The Christian today is to remain vigilant, waiting faithfully for the return of his Master. Luke 12:37, 38.

C. **The second coming is the great transition.**

The second coming of Christ means the end of sin and death for the believers. It means that all His followers will obtain the glorious promise of eternal life on a new earth. It is the great transition to which believers of all ages have been looking forward, praying, "Thy kingdom come." It is the moment to which all other beings in the unnumbered galaxies of the universe have been looking with joyful expectancy. It is the time when the redeemed sons of God of this earth will join them as loyal citizens of God's kingdom. The disciples of Jesus Christ and early Christians looked forward with eager expectation to this great day. Matthew 24:2, 3; Titus 2:13.

D. **Jesus comes to execute judgment.**

The second coming of Jesus Christ as King of kings is an integral part of God's plan of redemption for mankind, made before creation. At His first coming Jesus atoned for every man's sins through His death on the cross, thus making those who accept Him righteous. Every man is offered this great salvation from sin and death. By receiving Jesus Christ as his Lord and Saviour a man passes from death to life. Jesus Christ leads us to forsake sin, to hate our sinful natures, and to obey from the heart the commandments of God.

Men are now being invited to follow Christ until His return. When He comes, they will receive either reward or punishment, depending on their decisions made in this life. The great question for us is this: Are we allowing Jesus Christ to dwell in us? Christ will finish His plan of salvation by destroying sin and unrepentant sinners and by taking all those who have followed Him to the new earth. 2 Thessalonians 1:7-10.

II. THE GREAT HOPE OF THE SCRIPTURES IS CHRIST'S RETURN

A. How is Jesus coming the second time?

1. He will come in the same way as He went to heaven. Acts 1:9-11. Everyone will see Him. Revelation 1:7. He will come as lightning. Matthew 24:27.
2. There will be a great sound. Matthew 24:31.
3. He will come in indescribable glory. Matthew 25:30.
4. He will come suddenly, surprising us all. Matthew 24:42, 44.

B. What will He do at that time?

1. He will raise the righteous dead and take them to heaven. 1 Thessalonians 4:16, 17.
2. He will transform the living righteous and take them to heaven. 1 Corinthians 15:51, 52.
3. He will destroy the unrighteous. Jude 14, 15; 2 Thessalonians 2:8.

C. We must be ready for His second coming.

1. After he has given himself to Jesus, the believer abides in Him. 1 John 2:28.
2. He has fellowship with the Holy Spirit every moment of the day. John 14:17, 26. He is in touch with God through prayer and Bible study.
3. He dies daily to sin. He is willing to die to his selfish nature, and he allows Jesus Christ, through the Holy Spirit, to reign in him. 2 Corinthians 5:15; 1 Corinthians 15:31.
4. He allows Jesus to change him into His likeness. 1 John 3:2, 3.
5. He expects Jesus to return any time. Titus 2:12, 13.
6. He loves Jesus and looks forward to His return. 2 Timothy 4:8.

D. Satan's aim is to keep men in ignorance and unpreparedness.

Satan does everything in his power to discourage man's hope in the imminent return of Jesus Christ. His aim is to make the idea of Christ's return look absurd and ridiculous. Thereby he hopes that people will not believe in this great event and will not be ready for it.

Those who are eagerly expecting Jesus also have to expect difficulties from Satan, since he attempts to prevent them from being ready at Christ's coming. Men can give mental assent to the doctrine of Christ's return and not be spiritually ready for His coming. Christ mentioned this possibility by telling the parable of the ten virgins. Matthew 25:1-13. All ten virgins believed that the bridegroom would come, but only five were received by Him. Why? Because only five were prepared; only five had the indwelling Christ. What would be your fate if Jesus Christ were to return tonight? Are you prepared?

The expectation of the imminent return of Jesus Christ should be a great encouragement to everyone to surrender himself to Christ every day, to make certain that there is spiritual growth in his life, and that by Christ's power he is overcoming his evil nature.

III. SIGNIFICANT PARALLELS BETWEEN JEWISH AND CHRISTIAN HISTORY

A. The difference between Christ's first and second advents.

Both the first and the second coming of Jesus were prophesied in the Holy Scriptures. The Jewish nation expected the promised Messiah but made a fatal error in its interpretation of prophecy. It failed to see that these are two separate events. The Bible makes plain the difference.

1. Christ's first coming was in humility and poverty to suffer and to die as the Lamb of God, taking away the sin of the world. He came to pay the penalty of sin, which is the second death (or hell), and to establish His spiritual kingdom of grace. He came to enlist men as His disciples and to call subjects to His kingdom. All those who voluntarily accept Him as their Saviour and are willing to accept His principles as their standard of life receive forgiveness of their sins and obtain His righteousness. They will enter the kingdom of God. Isaiah 53:5, 7; John 1:29; 18:37.

2. His second coming will be in great power and glory as the King of kings, to execute judgment. He will take to heaven His redeemed people, and make forever an end to the dominion of sin and death.

B. The Jews made a tragic mistake.

The Jews were expecting the appearance of the Messiah, but they expected Him as a mighty king who would sit on the throne of David. They desired Him to drive out the Romans, subdue the heathen nations, and make Israel a great and powerful people. Their fatal mistake consisted in the fact that they did not recognize in the lowly Nazarene the fulfillment of the prophecies about the Messiah. They were greatly disturbed by His lack of political action. They resented His preaching of the gospel to the poor and to the sinners. They became very indignant when He exposed the hypocrisy of the "religionists." The humble resignation of Jesus and His willingness to suffer repulsed them; and they finally despised, ridiculed, rejected, and condemned Him to death in the name of God. Satan succeeded in blinding their eyes to the identity of the Lord of glory.

C. **Satan is using a similar strategy against Christians.**

1. The successful deceiver of Israel is applying the same strategy in the Christian era. He is having great success in deceiving the whole world. Revelation 12:9. He has succeeded in discrediting the promise of the second coming of Christ in the minds of many Christians. Although they rejoice over Christ's first coming as the Saviour and believe in His death and resurrection, they give no importance to the teaching of His second coming. They are vague regarding the purpose of His second coming and are not preparing their lives for the day when they will stand before the Son of man. "Watch ye therefore, and pray always, that ye may be accounted worthy to escape all these things that shall come to pass, and to stand before the Son of man." Luke 21:36.

2. The Jewish leaders and the nation expected the Messiah to come in glory; they were not aware of the fact that first He had to come as the suffering servant of God to die for the sins of mankind. They misinterpreted Biblical prophecies regarding His second coming and applied them to His first coming. They were ignorant of the two separate events in God's plan of redemption. Many Christians make a similar error. They are concerned only with Christ's first coming and are not preparing for His second coming. Revelation 6:15-17.

   Pray that you may be among that small minority who are aware of the imminence of the Messiah's return, and that you may eagerly expect Him. Continuous preparedness for this event is a matter of life and death for all of us. 1 Thessalonians 5:4, 5; 2 Timothy 4:8.

Significant World Events of Great Magnitude

INTRODUCTION

We consider ourselves to be primarily physical beings; we often speak of having five senses. The Holy Scriptures, however, claim that we also have a spiritual nature. We have been endowed with a sensitiveness for things that are spiritual. But we can be so carnally minded that our spiritual senses are dulled or out of order. Jesus Christ referred to this state in man when He said, "This people's heart is waxed gross, and their ears are dull of hearing, and their eyes they have closed; lest at any time they should see with their eyes, and hear with their ears, and should understand with their heart, and should be converted, and I should heal them." Matthew 13:15.

The Pharisees had keen minds, but they were spiritually blind. Their thorough theological education did not help them correct this situation. From early morning until late at night they followed Jesus Christ, watching and studying Him carefully. They witnessed His miracles and were astonished at the way He healed the sick and raised the dead. Nevertheless, they asked Him: "Teacher, we wish to see a sign from You." Matthew 12:38, RSV. "What sign do You do, that we may see, and believe You? What work do You perform?" John 6:30, RSV.

The many miracles Jesus performed were not acceptable to them as signs of divine authority; they demanded a special sign, one that should be done according to their own liking. This reminds us of Satan who approached Christ in the wilderness and challenged Him, "If Thou be the Son of God, command that these stones be made bread." Matthew 4:3.

The Pharisees demanded of Jesus a spectacular sign like the one Joshua received when the sun stood still over Beth-horon. The humble shepherds of Bethlehem, the three wise kings from the East, received such a spectacular sign without having asked for it. They beheld the star of Bethlehem in the heavens, but the proud rabbis were not given this privilege.

The greatest sign of all was Jesus Christ Himself, His wonderful character, His mighty words and deeds. "Behold, this Child is set for the fall and rising again of many in Israel; and for a sign which shall be spoken against." Luke 2:34. When Jesus saw that the religious leaders of the nation refused to accept His signs, He answered, "This is an evil generation: they seek a sign; and there shall no sign be given it, but the sign of Jonas the prophet." Luke 11:29.

I. SPIRITUAL BLINDNESS HAS TERRIBLE RESULTS

A. None are so blind as those who refuse to see.

Many people are spiritually blind; they cannot understand spiritual lessons. It is not sufficient to see the signs God gives us; we must also understand their significance. The Word of God explains clearly the significance of world events and the signs given to us by God. The Holy Scripture provides us with a divine exegesis of past history, of present events, and of earth-shattering happenings in the future which should make men's hearts tremble. But do we understand what we read?

B. Stubbornness can lead to spiritual blindness.

Jesus reproached the rabbis in these words: "O ye hypocrites, ye can discern the face of the sky; but can ye not discern the signs of the times?" Matthew 16:3. These men were not able to perceive the significance of the times they were living in; they did not know that certain events taking place then contained deep spiritual significance.

Someone brought to Jesus the news of the slaughter of a number of Galilean men. They were killed in the temple, and Pilate's soldiers had mixed their blood with blood from animal sacrifices. When hearing of this tragedy Jesus told them, "Suppose ye that these Galileans were sinners above all the Galileans, because they suffered such things? I tell you, Nay: but, except ye repent, ye shall all likewise perish." Luke 13:2, 3. In other words, Jesus called their attention to the fact that this event was a sign of much greater calamities to come.

He gave His listeners a prophetic glance into the future when Jerusalem should be besieged and captured by Roman armies. He knew that hundreds of thousands of people would perish, and that their blood would flow freely in the temple courts. However, the people did not understand; they did not know the time of their visitation. They did not perceive in Christ's words a warning, a call to repent, and they did not take refuge in Him. According to Josephus, more than a million people perished in the siege of Jerusalem. See Luke 19:41-44.

C. **The destruction of Jerusalem is a symbol of the destruction of the world.**

The disciples were greatly perplexed when Jesus told them of the coming destruction of the temple. Matthew 23:38; 24:1, 2. They could not believe that this magnificent temple would be leveled to the ground. They asked Him to give them some sure sign pointing to this event. Matthew 24:3. In His reply Jesus pointed to several great future events:

1. The destruction of Jerusalem and of the temple.
2. The end of the world.
3. His glorious second coming.

The destruction of Jerusalem was an example and a prophetic symbol of the destruction of the world which will occur at the time of Christ's second coming.

"Everything in the world is in agitation. The signs of the times are ominous. . . . There are those who are waiting and watching and working for our Lord's appearing. Another class are falling into line under the generalship of the first great apostate. Few believe with heart and soul that we have a hell to shun and a heaven to win.

"The crisis is stealing gradually upon us. . . . The highest excitement prevails, yet probation's hour is fast closing, and every case is about to be eternally decided." —*The Desire of Ages,* page 636.

D. **Obedience to Christ's signs means deliverance.**

In Matthew 24:4-44 Jesus Christ gave a prophetic proclamation which contained the signs of His second coming. In this prophecy He spoke both of the destruction of the Jewish nation and of the destruction of the world; of the deliverance of the first Christians during the great massacre in Jerusalem and of the deliverance of Christ's remnant people at the end of the world. These signs were of great importance to the Christians living in the first century, since many of them narrowly escaped the destruction of Jerusalem; the same chapter is speaking today to this generation which is faced with the stupendous climax of world history: the return of Jesus Christ.

Many religious people in the time of Christ could see only the approach of great national prosperity; in the same way, multitudes of Christians today interpret the prophecies regarding the return of Jesus Christ as tokens of unprecedented progress and peace on earth.

The true Christians living in the first century, on the other hand, heeded Christ's warning. When Cestius, the Roman general, temporarily withdrew his army from the walls of Jerusalem, the Christians immediately took flight to Perea. Shortly afterward the Roman armies under Titus returned to besiege and capture the city. Not one of these Christians perished, because they had heeded Christ's warning. The same principle applies to believers today. The signs of Christ's coming are to warn us of impending danger.

II. THESE SIGNS APPEAR IN OUR TIMES

A. Signs in the political world.

1. Distress, fear, and perplexity. Luke 21:25-27.
2. World wars, widespread famines, pestilences, and earthquakes. The prophecies refer mainly to the magnitude of these catastrophes rather than their frequency. Matthew 24:5-7; Revelation 11:18.
3. The failure of all efforts to establish world peace. In spite of the "Palais de Paix" in the Hague, the League of Nations in Geneva, and the United Nations in New York, there is no prospect of world peace. 1 Thessalonians 5:1-3.

B. Signs in the breakup of the fabric of society.

Nineteen hundred years ago the apostle Paul foresaw the numerous characteristics of the social life of our time with startling clarity and exactness. 2 Timothy 3:1-5.

C. Signs in the economic world.

Struggles between capital and labor, loss of personal holdings. James 5:1-9.

D. Signs in the field of science.

Staggering achievements in science, technology, and industry follow in quick succession. While scientific developments surpass expectations, man is becoming spiritually and morally decadent. See Daniel 12:4.

E. Signs in the religious and spiritual spheres of our time.

1. Men ridicule the teaching of Christ's second coming. 2 Peter 3:3, 4.
2. People are outwardly religious but inwardly empty of genuine spiritual power. 2 Timothy 3:1, 5.
3. The love of pleasure and entertainment are more sought after than is the love of God. 2 Timothy 3:4.
4. There is little Biblical faith left on earth. Luke 18:8.
5. Sin and selfishness pervade the hearts of men. Genuine love and affection are rare. Matthew 24:12.
6. The everlasting gospel and the message of Christ's return are proclaimed for a witness, on a worldwide scale. No man can honestly say that he has never

been confronted with some element of God's revelation. Romans 1:20.

F. **Signs in the sky.**

God uses signs in the sky to shed light on certain events on earth. Genesis 1:14; Matthew 24:29, 30; Joel 3:15.

1. The sun was darkened (not by an eclipse) on May 19, 1780; that night the moon was darkened and then changed in color.

2. The stars fell on November 13, 1833—the most spectacular and long-continued meteoric shower of which we have record.

III. CHRIST WARNS THE LAST GENERATION

A. **Jesus requires preparation and readiness.**

These are the words of Jesus Christ to us who live in the time of His return, "Take ye heed, watch and pray; for ye know not when the time is." Mark 13:33. This means that we are not to be spiritually asleep, lest Christ find us unprepared. "As the days of Noah were, so shall also the coming of the Son of man be." Matthew 24:37. "But of that day and hour knoweth no man." Verse 36. "When ye shall see all these things, know that it is near, even at the doors." Verse 33.

Jesus did not give us the exact time of His second coming. He merely described the conditions on earth during the last period of the world's history. He instructs us to be prepared at all times, to live every day as if He were to arrive suddenly. This spirit of readiness keeps us spiritually alert. Only then will we be prepared for His return. Matthew 24:42.

B. **Christians face the same dangers as did the Jews.**

Christ warned this last generation in the same manner as He warned His contemporaries of the destruction of Jerusalem. Unfortunately most of us today have the same reaction to these warnings as the Jews did in their time. Few of us recognize the time of our visitation.

Few see these events in the light of prophetic statements. As a result, we do not obey these warnings, and think we are not responsible for our unpreparedness. Only a few Christians are aware of the imminence of His return. "Ye, brethren, are not in darkness. . . . Therefore let us not sleep, as do others." 1 Thessalonians 5:4-6.

Do not postpone the date of your conversion. Feeble resistance against your sinful habits is not sufficient. You need the divine power of Jesus Christ and the Holy Spirit in overcoming your sinful nature. In the parable of the ten virgins all were waiting for the bridegroom, but only five were ready. The other five were lost. "And they that were ready went in with him." Matthew 25:10. Do not tolerate any hindrance in your life which has a tendency to postpone your preparation. Readiness means being justified by the life and death of Jesus Christ, being born anew by His Holy Spirit, being transformed by the indwelling Holy Spirit into the image of Jesus Christ. Only when you have evidence that these things have taken place in your lives will you have the assurance that you will stand before the Judge of all men robed in the white garments of Christ's righteousness. Titus 3:5-7.

C. **Blessed are the eyes which can see.**

We live in a grand and awful time. Signs of the greatest magnitude are telling with unmistakable voice of the coming of the Lord of glory. He who has eyes shall see, and he who has ears shall listen to what these portentous signs are telling. Sin is riding high. Demon-possessed men are making life on earth unsafe and unbearable. The Spirit of God is gradually withdrawing from earth. It is a great privilege to be aware of coming events. Shall we who know the plans of God from the Holy Scriptures and understand the significance of the signs in the world keep silent? Impossible! With loving hearts and with great compassion for our fellowmen, we must urge them to wake up and ask Christ to save their lives. Luke 12:37.

God's Schedule of Events

INTRODUCTION

Jesus Christ is the center of our salvation. The plan of salvation was conceived in detail in the secret council of the Godhead before creation. Zechariah 6:13; 1 Peter 1:20. Jesus Christ, the Son of God, has been carrying out this glorious plan of salvation for mankind in a most wonderful and victorious way. The whole universe is watching the progress of His divine plan.

When mankind became rebellious and morally decadent, God destroyed it through a flood. He saved Noah and his family who had been faithful to Him. Through them He populated the earth again. The salvation of that family during that great catastrophe was a symbol of the miraculous redemption of mankind.

When Jesus Christ died on the cross, He paid the price for saving all mankind from sin; He made a final atonement for all who had faith in Him. Our salvation from sin was finished on the cross of Calvary, while other phases of God's plan of salvation, such as Christ's second advent, are still waiting to be fulfilled.

I. THE ALPHA AND OMEGA OF GOD'S PLAN OF SALVATION IS JESUS CHRIST

A. "I have trodden the wine press alone; . . . there was none with Me." Isaiah 63:3.

In this lesson we will dwell on a phase of God's plan of salvation that remains yet to be fulfilled. The center and chief figure in God's plan of redemption is the Son of God, our Saviour. He has begun the redemption of mankind and will also finish it victoriously. He is the Alpha and Omega, the beginning and the end of our faith, the very center of attraction. Revelation 1:8.

B. Salvation is the greatest of all sciences.

The science of salvation is the deepest study man can undertake in this world; even angels desire to understand it more fully. It will be the theme of study for the redeemed throughout eternity when the secrets of God will be opened before their eyes. The far-reaching consequences of this plan of salvation will be felt by all.

Every man on this earth should be familiar with this plan and should be able to give an intelligent explanation of it. This science should have priority in the education of all young people. This science is the most important subject, not only for the theologians but also for all other sinners. It is as much a "must" as is the knowledge of reading and writing.

C. Several phases of the plan of salvation are still to be fulfilled.

The phases to be fulfilled deal with the second coming of Jesus Christ to take the redeemed to heaven, and with our return with Him to the earth after the millennium. Let us study God's schedule for these events and familiarize ourselves with His course of action as explained in the Holy Scriptures.

II. A THOUSAND YEARS OF CHAOS AND RUIN
A. A diagram of the millennium.

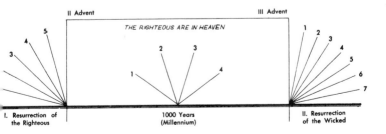

B. **Mistaken ideas about the millennium are widespread.**

The word "millennium" means 1,000 years. Theologians have advanced a number of erroneous concepts regarding this period of time. Many sincere Christians mistakenly believe that the second coming of Christ will initiate the Golden Age of mankind on earth, a time when all men will be converted to God, when nations will not wage war, when everlasting peace and happiness will prevail. This is not based on sound Scriptural exegesis.

There are theologians who expect the second coming of Christ to occur before the millennium. These are called premillennialists. Those who expect Him to come after the millennium are called postmillennialists. Believers in the "secret rapture" teach that Jesus Christ will come secretly for His chosen ones seven years before the millennium. This premise also lacks Biblical foundation. Read Revelation 20:1-9, where we find God's explanation of the chief events concerning the millennium.

C. **These events occur at the beginning of the millennium. (See diagram under A.)**
   1. Jesus Christ returns the second time. His return is visible to all men; He will not come down to the earth but will remain visible in the sky as described by Paul in 1 Thessalonians 4:15-18.
   2. All the righteous dead since the time of Adam are resurrected. This is called the first resurrection. Revelation 20:6.
   3. The unrighteous, those who have rejected Jesus Christ, will be destroyed. 2 Thessalonians 1:7-9.
   4. The resurrected righteous dead and the righteous living at that time receive a new body and go to heaven with Jesus. 1 Thessalonians 4:16, 17; Philippians 3:21.
   5. Satan is bound by inactivity. Revelation 20:2, 3.

D. **These events take place during the millennium. (See diagram under A.)**
   1. The earth is in a chaotic condition resembling its

state on the first day of creation. Revelation 20:3; Isaiah 24:3, 19, 20.

2. All the unrighteous humans are dead. Revelation 6:15-17; 19:17-19, 21.

3. Satan is inactive for 1,000 years because there are no living human beings on earth to tempt and control. Revelation 20:2.

4. The righteous people are in heaven; together with Christ they are judging fallen angels and the unrighteous dead. Revelation 20:4; 1 Corinthians 6:1-3.

E. **These events take place at the end of the millennium. (See diagram under A.)**

1. Jesus Christ descends upon the Mount of Olives. Zechariah 14:4, 5.

2. The New Jerusalem, with the redeemed righteous, descends from heaven. Revelation 21:2.

3. All the unrighteous since the time of Cain are resurrected. Revelation 20:5, first part.

4. Satan is released from his inactivity. Having regained his subjects, he continues his work of deception among the unrighteous. Revelation 20:7.

5. Satan organizes the unrighteous to attack the New Jerusalem, the Holy City, in order to make it their own. Revelation 20:8, 9.

6. Fire descends from heaven and utterly destroys Satan, the fallen angels, and the unrighteous. Revelation 20:9.

7. Jesus Christ creates a new earth and a new heaven for the righteous. Revelation 21:1-5.

This is the breathtaking plan of God for mankind. It should change our whole outlook on life. With absolute precision the plan is being carried out by God, in spite of satanic and human attempts to hinder it. The authority, the honor, and the glory of God are committed to its accomplishment.

To conform to God's plan means life; to reject or oppose it means death.

World History Foretold in a Metallic Statue

INTRODUCTION

Jesus Christ, the Son of God, is our Creator and Redeemer, but He is also overseeing human history and controlling the destinies of peoples, nations, and individuals. "He changeth the times and the seasons; He removeth kings, and setteth up kings." Daniel 2:21. "It is not in man's power as he walks to control his steps." Jeremiah 10:23, Smith and Goodspeed.

I. **HISTORY REVEALS HOW GOD CONTROLS EVENTS**
   A. **The Bible explains the philosophy of history.**
      The destiny of people and of nations is not shaped by the whim and ambition of men but by the will of God, who directs human history with a firm hand.

      Nation after nation is allowed to appear on the world stage and play its role. It takes sides either with truth and goodness or with error and wickedness. It either fulfills its Heaven-appointed calling or rejects it. Many a nation, by oppressing, conquering, and exploiting other nations, rejecting God and His principles, and causing much sorrow and misery to its people, has abused the power it has received from God.

      To a certain extent God allows Satan, who is called the prince of this world, a free hand to achieve his purpose, but He sets up a boundary which Satan is not permitted to cross. He is allowed to demonstrate his rebellion only to the extent permitted by God. A superficial study of history might lead one to the conclusion that the destiny of nations and individuals is entirely governed by the will of powerful rulers and tyrants, or is meaningless, or is controlled by deterministic fates. We have sufficient evidence from the Word of God, however, that the unseen hand of God is overruling the kings and lords of this earth, and that in the end God accomplishes His purpose in history. Empire after empire has emerged, prospered, and then spent itself. Other nations followed, occupied their place, and then vanished again. World history is a testimony to the fact that God is righteous and that He rules this world in righteousness.

B. **The apostle Peter mentions three worlds in his epistles.**
   1. The world that existed before the great Flood. 2 Peter 3:5, 6.
   2. The present world reserved for destruction by fire. 2 Peter 3:7.
   3. The new world to come, in which dwells righteousness. 2 Peter 3:13.

C. **God can use any nation as His tool to fulfill His mighty purpose in the present world.**
   Although heathen nations have rejected the true God, He still uses them to fulfill His purpose. For example, God often used godless nations to punish His people, the Israelites, in order to teach them a lesson.

   Let us examine the role of heathen nations in world history. Let us see how God suddenly interfered with the life of some of the most brutal nations in the world, such as Babylon, which was the world headquarters for paganism and idolatry: it was the very symbol of heathen worship. Babylon became a conquerer of Israel. It actually captured the chosen people of God, destroyed Jerusalem, and took the people into captivity. How did God use this mighty nation for His purpose?

II. A GREAT DRAMA IS REVEALED IN A DREAM TO THE KING

A. Daniel rescues the king's advisers from capital punishment.

The king of Babylon, Nebuchadnezzar, had taken Daniel and his three companions, who were all members of leading Jewish families, as captives to Babylon, together with multitudes of other Jews. One night Nebuchadnezzar had a disturbing dream; in the morning he was alarmed because he could not remember this dream. He asked his astrologers and advisers to tell him his dream and give him its interpretation. When they confessed that they were unable to do so, the king commanded that they be executed. Daniel 2:3, 10, 11, 13.

Daniel approached the king and asked him for time and for an opportunity to reveal the dream to him. Daniel and his three Hebrew friends fasted and prayed to God for light. Their lives were at stake. God revealed the fateful dream to Daniel and gave him its interpretation. Daniel 2:19-22. When telling the dream to the king, Daniel informed him that the God who made heaven and earth, who sets up and removes kings, who changes times and seasons, who limits the expansion of every empire, had revealed to the king through this dream the development of human history in advance, starting with the Babylonian Empire and ending with God's kingdom, the new earth. The new earth was to be God's own empire, set up in His own time. Daniel 2:28, 29, 44.

B. Daniel gives the dream and its interpretation.

We cannot think of anything more exciting for a historian to read than the second chapter of the book of Daniel, which is a divine prophecy of some of the events of world history. If it is found to correspond with the developments of world history, then any thinking man should realize that God is the Governor and Lord of world history.

The dream itself is recounted in Daniel 2:31-35, and its interpretation is given in Daniel 2:36-45.

C. **History developed exactly as foretold by God through Daniel.**

Let us briefly observe the succession of the different empires described here:

1. The gold head stood for Babylon.
2. In 539 B.C. the Medo-Persian kingdom took the power away from Babylon.
3. Later, the Greek king, Alexander the Great, conquered Persia in the battle of Arbela, 331 B.C.
4. The iron hand of Rome conquered the divided Greek kingdoms, the last one in 161 B.C. at the battle of Pydna.
5. Rome ruled until her crumbling empire was divided among ten kings in the fifth century A.D. These ten kings corresponded with the ten toes of the statue in King Nebuchadnezzar's dream.
6. The ten main divisions are the Alemanni (Germans); the Franks (French); the Burgundians (Swiss); the Suevi (Portuguese); the Saxons (English); the Visigoths (Spanish); the Lombards (Italians); the Heruli, the Vandals, and the Ostrogoths. These tribes made victorious invasions as early as A.D. 351. History gives A.D. 476 as the date of Rome's fall, when Emperor Augustulus (Little Augustus) was deposed. The modern nations of Europe developed from these barbarian tribes.

It is remarkable to note that the four empires described deteriorated in quality as symbolized by the head of gold (Babylon) and ended in mixed clay and iron (the ten barbarian tribes). According to prophecy, the divided nations of Europe would mix (through marriage), but they would never become one politically. In vain have such powerful men as Charlemagne, Louis XIV, Napoleon, Kaiser Wilhelm II, and Hitler tried to unite Europe politically. None of them have succeeded, since God ordered affairs contrary to their plans.

D. **The remaining part of the dream is still to be fulfilled.**

Daniel explained that a stone, not cut out by human hands, would break the statue. This means that the divided kingdoms reigning to the end of world history will be replaced by God's own kingdom, which shall never be destroyed. Daniel 2:44, 45. God will destroy every nation and empire and establish a new earth governed by Him. The Bible explains how the last part of Nebuchadnezzar's dream will be fulfilled. It speaks of the establishment of God's own kingdom in these words: "The kingdoms of this world are become the kingdoms of our Lord, and of His Christ; and He shall reign forever and ever." Revelation 11:15. "And the nations were angry, and Thy wrath is come." Verse 18. "Ten kings . . . receive power as kings one hour with the beast." Revelation 17:12. "He hath on His vesture . . . a name written, King of kings, and Lord of lords." "And out of His mouth goeth a sharp sword, that with it He should smite the nations." Revelation 19:16, 15. "The spirits of devils . . . gather them to the battle of that great day of God Almighty." Revelation 16:14. "Come and gather yourselves together unto the supper of the great God." Revelation 19:17.

E. **The Bible provides the only true philosophy of history.**

The greatest part of this prophecy, given 2,600 years ago, has been fulfilled. History attests to the truthfulness of this divine prophecy revealed in a human statue. Today we are standing on the threshhold of the last event: the falling of the great stone which was not cut by human hands.

In vain do we study the facts of history if we are not familiar with the reasons why these events occurred. The true meaning of history is found in the Holy Scriptures, where God's hand is seen clearly in the affairs of men. At the same time, we see the evil plans of Satan in his attempts to counteract God's actions; we are fascinated to see that in spite of all Satanic and human opposition God is accomplishing His purpose in the end. We learn through the rise and fall of great nations how transitory all earthly glory and riches are and that only those things remain forever that are built on God and on His principles.

III. JESUS CHRIST, THE LORD OF HISTORY, IS THE COMING KING

A. **The symbols in Holy Scripture point to Jesus Christ.**
1. The Second Person of the Godhead, the Son of God, is the Lord of history. It is He who removes kings and sets up kings. Daniel 2:20, 21. "Remove the diadem, and take off the crown. . . . I will overturn, overturn, overturn, it: . . . until He come whose right it is." Ezekiel 21:26, 27. Jesus Christ is earth's rightful Ruler.
2. What spirit inspired prophets such as Daniel to write these prophecies? "Holy men of God spake as they were moved by the Holy Ghost." 2 Peter 1:21. "What manner of time the Spirit of Christ which was in them did signify." 1 Peter 1:11.
3. What is symbolized by that falling stone which was cut without human hands? That stone is Jesus Christ as He returns in power and glory, putting a sudden end to all the kingdoms of this earth. Jesus asked us to pray for this great event: "Thy kindgom come." Matthew 6:10. "Whosoever shall fall on this stone shall be broken: but on whomsoever it shall fall, it will grind him to powder." Matthew 21:44.

B. **Jesus Christ measures the peoples of this earth in the balance.**

We have been looking at a prophetic picture of world history given 2,600 years ago. We can only stand in awe and admiration of God's foreknowledge of these events. Jesus said that heaven and earth will pass away but His words shall not. Matthew 24:35. He is the Lord of world history, and He will be the great Judge of all people, weighing every one of us carefully in the balance, saying to the lost, "Mene, mene, tekel, upharsin," which means among other things that they have been weighed in the balance and have come up short. Daniel 5:25, 27. God has given us the forecast of world history for our benefit that we may understand more intelligently the developments of the history of man and make our decisions wisely. Jesus said, "And when these things begin to come to pass, then look up." "Watch ye therefore, and pray always, that ye may be accounted worthy to escape all these things that shall come to pass, and to stand before the Son of man." Luke 21:28, 36.

C. **Jesus will come for you.**

Man of God, take a look at the world clock; soon it will strike again and time will be gone forever. Set in order your life with Jesus Christ and your fellowman.

The four empires described appeared on the world scene and are gone. Seven of the ten kingdoms (the divided European nations) have been here for over a thousand years, and soon the last part of this great prophecy will be fulfilled as scheduled. As soon as the clock of the world strikes for the last time, the King of kings will come to judge the living and the dead and to establish His rightful empire. History testifies to the fact that the dream originated with God and that its interpretation is absolutely accurate.

Nebuchadnezzar, the proud king, had to learn through bitter humiliation that God rules over the kingdoms of men. Daniel 4:17, 35. In the same manner all earthly rulers will be humbled before Jesus Christ.

Where do you stand today? Whose side have you taken in the great controversy between Christ and Satan? We pray that at the return of Jesus Christ you will say: "Lo, this is our God; we have waited for Him, and He will save us." Isaiah 25:9.

World History Foretold in Symbols of Beasts

INTRODUCTION

Few people realize that behind the great historical developments of the world is a sharp controversy, with God and His Messiah on one hand and the nations of earth on the other. This spiritual battle has been raging since the time of Cain and Abel and will not end until Jesus returns. This spiritual battle will actually become more intensified and violent as time goes on toward the climax.

I. THE NATIONS, PEOPLES, AND KINGS ARE ARRAYED AGAINST JESUS CHRIST, THE MESSIAH

A. The Bible contains the key to the understanding of history.

1. The mysterious antagonism of nations (both heathen and "Christian") against God in the course of history is illuminated by a statement in Psalm 2:1-4: "Why do the heathen rage, and the people imagine a vain thing? The kings of the earth set themselves, and the rulers take counsel together, against the Lord, and against His Anointed, saying, Let us break Their bands asunder, and cast away Their cords from us. He that sitteth in the heavens shall laugh: the Lord shall have them in derision." The same thought is expressed in Psalm 59:8.

   These texts reveal the opposition of the nations

throughout the history of the world against the mighty God, His Anointed, His commandments, His plans, and His principles. See also Acts 4:25-27, where Peter applies Psalm 2:1-4 to Jesus Christ.

2. Of Jesus it is said, "He came unto His own, and His own received Him not." John 1:11. This statement gives us an idea of the enmity in the heart of the Israelites against the Messiah. Jesus was well aware of it and referred to it in a parable. "His citizens hated him, and sent a message after him, saying, We will not have this man to reign over us." Luke 19:14.

B. **Nation after nation turned against God.**

1. God rules over the seas; He also rules over the nations of the earth. As He calms the stormy waves of the sea, so He calms the angry agitations of nations. Psalm 65:7. He brings their counsel to naught. Psalm 33:10, 11. The nations are generally not aware of the activities of God in their affairs. They believe that it is human power, ambition, fortune, the whim of rulers, that determine the fate of nations and empires. They do not perceive the hand of God in the affairs of men. God once revealed His presence very dramatically, when He wrote on the walls of a king's palace the words "Mene, mene, tekel, upharsin," meaning in part, "You have been weighed in the scales of heaven and found wanting." That same night the kingdom was overthrown by an enemy. Still, few rulers have ever acknowledged the supremacy of God in their affairs.

2. In every generation God permits nations to make their choice for or against Him. As with individuals, He respects their free will and gives them the opportunity to make their own choice. God does not coerce people to follow Him or to live according to His principles, even if the course they choose leads them to destruction. "In past generations He allowed

all the nations to walk in their own ways."
Acts 14:16, RSV.

II. GOD FORECASTS SUCCEEDING WORLD EMPIRES

A. Daniel revealed the history of mankind as God sees it.

Jesus Christ stressed the importance of Daniel's prophecy. Matthew 24:15. In the second chapter of the book of Daniel, God revealed to a heathen king the sequence of world empires until the end of the world. The symbol used was a human-like statue, as we saw in the previous lesson. In the seventh chapter of Daniel a startling new vision is recorded. It deals with the same succession of empires. This time their tyrannical nature is expressed in symbols of wild beasts. God was concerned that His followers should understand the nature of these world empires. For the sake of clarity He used two sets of symbols, a human-like statue and a group of wild beasts.

It is still common today for nations to be symbolized by animals. England is symbolized by a lion, Russia by a bear, the United States by an eagle, France by a rooster, China by a dragon, et cetera.

B. The prophecy mentions four empires and ten kingdoms.

Daniel's vision is described in Daniel 7:2-8, 13, 14, 26, 27. The symbolic language used in these verses is explained elsewhere in Scripture, for the Bible interprets itself.

1. Seas and water represent people and nations. Revelation 17:15.
2. Tornadoes and winds denote wars. Jeremiah 25:32, 33.
3. The four wild beasts represent four great empires. Daniel 7:17.
4. The lion with eagle's wings stands for Babylon. (Daniel 7 paralleled with Daniel 2.)
5. The bear symbolized Medo-Persia. (Daniel 7 paralleled with Daniel 2.)

6. The four-headed leopard represents the Greek empire which was divided into four parts after the death of Alexander the Great and the collapse of his empire. These four parts were: Egypt, ruled by Ptolemy; Syria and Persia under Seleucus; Thrace and Asia Minor ruled by Lysimachus; Macedonia and Greece under Cassander.

7. The fourth beast, a hideous monster, stood for heathen Rome, the worst power of all. It had a rapacious character.

8. The ten horns of the beast represent ten kingdoms into which the Roman Empire was divided in the fifth century. Seven of the ten are still with us as nations or parts of nations. Three–the Heruli, the Vandals, and the Ostrogoths–vanished at the rise of the "little horn." Daniel 7:8, 20, 24.

   Descendants of the seven remaining kingdoms can be found as significant elements of England, France, Germany, Switzerland, Spain, Portugal, and Italy. Kings and dictators have tried in vain to unite these nations but have never succeeded. According to prophecy, God will not allow this to happen. We know from history that a horn denotes power. Many aristocratic families in Europe had seven, nine, or eleven horns on their crowns.

C. **The mysterious "little horn" appears**.

   Heathen Rome was dissolved into ten kingdoms, as we have seen. According to prophecy, the power called the "little horn" could not emerge before the breakup of the Roman Empire had occurred. Once this had taken place, the little horn filled the political vacuum. In order to determine what is meant by the little horn, we have to study its characteristics as revealed in different parts of Scripture.

   1. It is a political power, since we read that it conquered three Arian nations, the Heruli, the Vandals, and the Ostrogoths. Daniel 7:8, 20, 24.

2. The little horn is said to have human eyes and a mouth uttering statements of great import. It is described as being farsighted, establishing rules and laws. It was to be mightier than its contemporaries. Daniel 7:8, 20.

3. It is also a religious power; it makes high-sounding statements against the Most High. Daniel 7:25; 2 Thessalonians 2:3, 4.

4. The little horn makes war against the saints of the Most High; it persecutes them bitterly, destroys and conquers them. It does this all in the name of God. Daniel 7:21, 25; John 16:2.

5. It thinks that it can change times and laws. Daniel 7:25. The only law that deals with time is the fourth commandment.

6. The people of God are given into its hand for a certain period of time: "A time, two times, and half a time." Daniel 7:25, RSV. A time meant a calendar year of 360 days. One prophetic day stands for a calendar year. Ezekiel 4:6. The time prophecy refers to 1,260 years, which is arrived at as follows:

1 time, 360 days, equals	360 years
2 times, 720 days, equals	720 years
1/2 time, or 180 days, equals	180 years
Total	1,260 years

D. The most astounding time prophecy in Scripture.

This particular time prophecy was given seven times by God and is contained in two prophetic books of the Bible, Daniel, and the Revelation. God expressed it three times in *years,* Daniel 7:25; 12:7; Revelation 12:14; twice in *months,* Revelation 11:2; 13:5; twice in *days,* Revelation 11:3; 12:6. Many theologians, historians, Bible students, and church leaders throughout the ages have concluded that this great time prophecy began in A.D. 538 and ended in 1798. According to them, the little horn stands for the power of the antichrist.

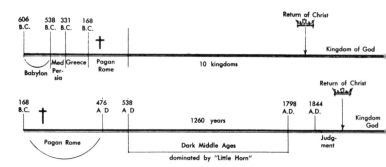

E. **The little horn will be judged and punished by God.**

The religio-political power symbolized by the little horn is said to rise to prominence again shortly before Christ's return. 2 Thessalonians 2:8. It will again be responsible for the persecution of God's people. God will judge it, take away its power, and finally destroy it. Daniel 7:26. Jesus Christ will then establish His kingdom on the new earth and give it to His people. Daniel 7:27. This corrupt power is called Babylon when it emerges at the end of history. Revelation 18:2, 5, 6.

III. **THE CONTROVERSY BETWEEN CHRIST AND THE NATIONS WILL COME TO AN END**
A. **Divine and human wrath will clash.**

Since the beginning of the world, kings and rulers have rebelled, raged, and counseled against God and His Messiah. They made every attempt to cast away His restraint and to break His control over them. See Psalm 2:1-4. The last generation on earth will carry this antagonism against God to an extreme, not realizing that by so doing it is invoking God's wrath upon itself. "Surely the wrath of man shall praise Thee: the remainder of wrath shalt Thou restrain." Psalm 76:10. "The nations were angry, and Thy wrath is come." Revelation 11:18.

B. **On which side are you?**

Did this brief study of prophecy give a clearer picture of the two opposing forces in this world? You should be able to see more through your spiritual eyes than through the eye of your body. Remember how Elisha the prophet saw the vast armies of God surrounding the enemy that was threatening the city of Dothan? "Open his eyes, that he may see." See 2 Kings 6:14-17. In the same manner, after the time of probation closes, two great armies will face each other. One will belong to Satan. It will be a human army arrayed against Jesus Christ, the Lamb of God. Revelation 16:14, 16; 17:12-14. The other army will belong to Jesus Christ. He will come to rescue His faithful followers who are being threatened by the satanic forces. Revelation 19:11, 15, 16; Joel 3:12, 14, 16.

This will be the last war on earth. It will be the settlement of all controversies between Christ with His following of redeemed sinners and Satan with his following of unrepentant men.

Today, the antagonism against Jesus Christ and His principles is developing in the world. In a short time the great mass of humanity, inspired by Satan and led by the antichrist, will prepare for war against the returning Christ. The result of this war will be terrible and devastating. Revelation 14:18-20; 19:17-19, 21. This will bring to an end the futile war of Satan and evil men against God which began in the Garden of Eden. It is the end of the great human tragedy.

When the opposers of Jesus Christ see the true Christ in all power and glory, who can stand against His wrath? See Revelation 6:15-17.

Those, on the other hand, who are siding with the true Christ will exclaim, "In the way of Thy judgments, O Lord, have we waited for Thee." Isaiah 26:8.

Judgment

The Bible has many references to the judgment of believers:

"The Lord shall judge His people." Hebrews 10:30.

"We must all appear before the judgment seat of Christ." 2 Corinthians 5:10.

"The time is come that judgment must begin at the house of God." 1 Peter 4:17, 18.

"The hour of His judgment is come." Revelation 14:7.

"Who will render to every man according to his deeds: to them who by patient continuance in well doing seek for glory and honor and immortality, eternal life: but unto them that are contentious, and do not obey the truth, . . . indignation and wrath." Romans 2:6-8.

"He that shall endure unto the end, the same shall be saved." Matthew 24:13.

The above texts show that God's judgment does not arbitrarily result in condemnation, but in many cases in God's approval.

Such a judgment or examination is taking place in heaven today. Genuine Christians will not be condemned in the judgment; nevertheless the record of their lives will be examined. The great grand jury of heaven is presently in session; and when the judgment of believers is finished, Jesus Christ will return.

All believers since Adam, whose names are written in the book of life, are being judged. The court of heaven examines whether the believer has accepted the light God has given him and has been willing to be conformed to the character of God.

God is revealing the life records of believers because He desires to demonstrate to the inhabitants of the universe that those who are going to be saved and those who will be rejected have been treated with infinite justice and love, and that every man is responsible for his own destiny.

Man lost his righteousness through the sin of Adam. The only way man can be saved is by obtaining the righteousness of Jesus Christ. The believer is offered this righteousness in two different ways: It is both imputed and imparted to him.

By "imputed" we mean that Jesus Christ not only forgives the sins of the believers by His blood on the cross, but also that He places the perfect record of His own life to the believer's account.

By "imparted" we mean that Jesus Christ, during the lifetime of the believer, dwells in him through the Holy Spirit. The Holy Spirit gradually changes the character of the believer until Christ's character is reproduced in him. It is the Holy Spirit who gives him the power to conform his life to the commandments of God.

There have always been believers who desired to receive Christ's imputed righteousness while refusing His imparted righteousness. They may not have it. God will not be mocked. Such persons show that they do not love Jesus sufficiently to desire to become like Him. They do not respect His commandments. The result is that such persons give the appearance of being Christians, but their actions contradict their words. Their old, sinful nature is still in control. They have not allowed Jesus Christ to reign in their hearts. They do not reflect the goodness and love of Christ in their daily lives. Such persons will not receive the imputed righteousness of Christ in the judgment. Jesus will not intercede for them. Their names will be removed from the book of life. They are condemned in spite of their claim to be believers.

Jesus Christ is the central figure of this judgment or examination. He has been the key figure in the unfolding and outworking of God's plan of salvation. Our human minds cannot grasp the full meaning of the work He has done for us. He is over all, God blessed forever. Romans 9:5. Christ is all and in all. Colossians 3:11. He is the fullness of the Godhead. Colossians 2:9. He is the Creator and Upholder of the universe. Colossians 1:15-17.

Christ is the Cornerstone of God's act of redemption. He is the Alpha and the Omega. Revelation 22:13. On the successful fulfillment of the plan of redemption depends the vindication of God's character. God could not have entrusted the outworking of His plan to anyone else. Only His Son could carry it out to completion.

Jesus Christ is the promised Lamb of God. John 1:36. He is the Saviour of mankind. Acts 5:31. When Christ ascended to heaven, He took with Him many believers whom He had resurrected as the firstfruits of His great victory over sin and death. Ephesians 4:8; Matthew 27:52, 53.

When He returned to heaven, Jesus received back the glory He had shared with His Father before His incarnation. John 17:5. He went to prepare a place for all believers. John 14:1-3. Christ became our only High Priest (Hebrews 4:15, 16), the only Mediator between man and God. 1 Timothy 2:5. Christ is in heaven to intercede for His saints and to hear and answer the prayers of all men who call on His name for salvation. Hebrews 7:25. He also sustains the entire universe by His power. Hebrews 1:3.

In the face of such a great God man can only bow down in humble adoration and worship.

This same Jesus is presently the central Figure of the judgment. He is the Judge, the Advocate of those whom He was permitted to indwell, and the King. John 5:22, 27; 1 John 2:1, 2; Revelation 19:16.

Human words are inadequate to express matters of such deep spiritual nature. God was gracious to give man a partial understanding of the great events taking place in heaven. Lessons 7 and 8 present what the Bible reveals to us regarding the finishing of the plan of salvation and the finishing of the mystery of God. Revelation 10:7. To God be glory forever and ever. Amen.

The Judgment Scene in Heaven

INTRODUCTION

In these last times the Holy Spirit has been gracious in shedding much light on the prophetic statements of the Bible dealing with God's judgment because these prophecies are being fulfilled. The judgment of God and the Biblical teaching regarding the heavenly temple are neglected themes. Many good Christians have never heard of them; nevertheless, they belong to the tenets and beliefs held by the Christian churches of the first century. These truths were lost over the centuries but now have been rediscovered and, like precious gems, are shining again in full light and glory as the church expects the imminent return of the Lord Jesus Christ.

I. GOD'S JUDGMENT OF BELIEVERS IS AS CERTAIN AS DEATH

A. We need an openness of mind.

Satan is the author of all error, prejudice, and false teaching. We need to guard against his efforts to blind our minds so that he will not succeed in keeping the message of God from us. He was most successful in keeping the religious leaders of Israel in the dark about the true Messiah. While they were sacrificing lambs in the temple in Jerusalem, the true Lamb of God was hanging on the cross outside the walls of the city. This was indeed a masterful deception by the enemy of God!

(49)

B. **The Old and the New Testaments complement each other.**

The book of Hebrews is to a large extent a parallel of two books in the Old Testament, Exodus and Leviticus. These three books shed light on God's temple in heaven, the heavenly sanctuary, where Jesus Christ, our High Priest, is ministering on our behalf. The book of Hebrews contains lessons pertaining to our era which we need to know. Let us delve into them prayerfully in the spirit of little Samuel when he said to God: "Speak; for Thy servant heareth." 1 Samuel 3:10.

C. **The atonement is part of God's plan of salvation.**

Jesus Christ atoned for our sins on the cross. No further sacrifice is necessary. He paid the full price of our salvation on Calvary. But God's plan of salvation which began in Eden did not end at Calvary; it finds its consummation in Eden restored on the new earth.

Today the world is still in rebellion against God; sin and death still take their toll. But Christians are looking forward to that glorious day when the heavens will open and Jesus will appear and take us into His presence. Some will be taken and some will be left.

God has chosen to reveal to the whole universe His justice in this choice. Of course, He could take the redeemed to heaven without giving anyone the reason for His selection, but God has ordained that the universe shall know why certain people will have this privilege.

God chose to disclose the records to show why these believers have been accepted by Him. He thinks that it is important for all unfallen beings in the universe to know why certain people have been selected.

It pleased God, through the prophet Daniel, to give mankind insight into His examination called the judgment in Daniel 7:10 and which we may appropriately call an examination of the books or the investigative judgment.

D. **Jesus Christ returns after the judgment is finished.**

When Jesus returns to earth, the destiny of every believer, dead or alive, is settled. 2 Corinthians 5:10. This is evident from Matthew 25:31-33: "When the Son of man shall come in His glory, . . . He shall separate them one from another, as a shepherd divideth his sheep from the goats: and He shall set the sheep on His right hand, but the goats on the left." From this passage it is clear that the destiny of every believer has been fixed beforehand in the examination in heaven, either for eternal life or for eternal death.

II. BIBLICAL EVIDENCE OF THE JUDGMENT
A. Both the Old and the New Testament point to it.

Paul states that if there is no law there is no sin. Romans 5:13. Obviously, if law does not provide a punishment for transgression then it loses its efficacy. In order to reach a verdict the cases of transgression are dealt with in a court. The Bible speaks of exactly such a court.

1. Both Paul and Peter refer to it. Acts 17:31; Romans 2:16; 1 Peter 4:17.
2. King Solomon mentions such an event in Ecclesiastes 12:14.
3. The basis of the judgment is the Ten Commandments. James 1:25; 2:12.
4. God will judge His people. Hebrews 10:30.
5. The judgment will separate believers into two groups. Romans 2:5-8.
6. We should be knowledgeable regarding God's judgment. Ecclesiastes 8:5.
7. God's judgment is in session now. Revelation 14:7.

The fourteenth chapter of Revelation describes a religious movement, symbolized by three angels flying through the air, which will appear on the world scene shortly before the return of Jesus Christ. This religious movement will call men's attention to the fact that God's judgment is come. The other interesting aspect of this movement is that it coincides with Daniel's prophecy of the beginning of the judgment: "Unto two thousand and three hundred days; then shall the sanctuary be cleansed." Daniel 8:14. The expression "the sanctuary be cleansed" refers to the examination of records, or the judgment in heaven. The expression "the sanctuary be cleansed" can only be properly understood after a careful study of the earthly tabernacle of Israel. The expression refers specifically to the work of the high priest on the yearly Day of Atonement. We will explain this service in more detail later on.

B. **The heavenly court is in session.**

"As I looked, thrones were placed. . . . The court sat in judgment, and the books were opened." Daniel 7:9, 10, RSV. This passage of Scripture describes the visions God gave His prophet Daniel regarding the judgment. God the Father is presiding, His angels are the witnesses, the book of deeds and the book of life are opened (Revelation 20:12), and every believer is judged.

The central figure of the judgment scene is Jesus Christ. He fills the functions of both Judge and Advocate. John 5:27; 1 John 2:1.

Christ is the Judge of all those believers whose records disclose that they have not loved Him sufficiently to be willing to be conformed by His power to His image; they have not asked for the indwelling Christ to give them the strength to keep the commandments of God. Believing in Christ to them meant a mental assent to a set of doctrines rather than a new love relationship with the Son of God. Jesus condemns such believers; their names are taken out of the book of life; their sins are not blotted out; and they face eternal death.

Christ is the Judge but also the Advocate of all those believers who love and obey Him with all their hearts and abide in Him to the end. Christ blots out their sins from the book of deeds by His own blood; He intercedes for them before the throne of the Father, and imputes His own righteousness to them. They are those who are saved by the grace of God through their faith in Jesus Christ. Ephesians 2:8; Revelation 3:5.

C. **The conclusion reached in the judgment.**

In the judgment all believers, starting with Adam and extending to all Christians until the return of the Lord, are being tried. 1 Peter 4:17, 18. When this work is finished Jesus Christ will cease to be our High Priest and the time of probation for humanity will come to a close. No one can be converted anymore; the Holy Spirit will be withdrawn from the world; there will be no longer a Mediator between God and man; there will be no more mercy extended to sinners. Revelation 15:5-8; 22:11. The plagues will fall on an unrepentant humanity, but the believers who have been accepted by God in the judgment will be spared. God will reveal His wrath toward all who have rejected His mercy. During the seventh plague Jesus Christ will return. Revelation 16:17.

D. **Jesus Christ referred to the judgment in a parable.**

Jesus points to the judgment of genuine and false believers in the parable of the king's wedding feast for his son. Matthew 22:2-10. The king examines the robes of the guests and rejects the one who does not have a wedding garment which symbolizes the righteous character of Jesus Christ. Matthew 22:11-13.

Through the centuries multitudes of people have heard God's invitation to enter His kingdom, but few have been willing to pay the price. The robes of the guests in the parable stand for the perfect character of Jesus Christ. Many believers have not been willing to deny self and be changed into the likeness of Christ. Because of their selfishness God has not been able to restore the divine image in them. They refused His transforming power and have tenaciously held on to their own views and character traits. Such believers are rejected in the judgment. Christ will not impute His righteousness to them.

Man cannot receive approval before the judgment seat of God clothed in his own goodness and righteousness. His best efforts to produce a perfect character fall short of the standard of God. Only Christ in us can fulfill God's requirements. The expressions "believing in Christ" and "receiving Christ" mean inviting Jesus to live His life in us.

Our characters reveal our affiliation and loyalties. Either Jesus Christ dwells within us so that we show forth His fruits in our daily lives, or else we are disguised agents of Satan revealing more and more of his evil nature.

III. HOW DOES GOD EXPECT US TO LIVE IN TIMES LIKE THIS?
A. We live on borrowed time.

Jesus Christ could have finished the judgment a long time ago if He had desired. It does not take God a hundred years to judge believers. But because of the angels and the unfallen beings of the universe God takes time to examine every case so that all intelligent beings may see His justice and grace in His verdicts. The reason He has delayed the finishing of the judgment is that in His great mercy He desires to give us as much time as possible to repent of our selfishness and return to Him. 2 Peter 3:9. Many Christians are lukewarm today and have not made a full surrender to Christ. Christ is not able to live in them, for they love rather than hate sin and the pleasures of the world. 1 John 2:15, 16.

If God were to close probation now, multitudes of professing Christians would be condemned. God is preparing for another worldwide revival. As He did at Pentecost, He is pouring out His Holy Spirit in an unusual measure on His faithful followers that they may proclaim Christ with divine power to perishing humanity for the last time. Christians of all churches will feel this convicting power of the Holy Spirit and realize their lost condition. They will become aware of the great apostasy sweeping through the Christian church today and will return to the Saviour and His teachings. People who are not members of any church will also hear the voice of Jesus through His faithful servants and accept God's invitation to enter His kingdom. They will gladly open their minds and hearts to the teachings of the Holy Scriptures and receive Jesus as the Master of their lives. Christians will be amazed to see the character of these converted worldlings changed in a brief time by the power of the indwelling Christ.

Now is the time of salvation; now the door of the kingdom of God is still wide open; now mercy is still in operation. Have you decided for or against receiving Christ? If you are a Christian, have you asked Jesus to come and live in you; or are you still the old, mean, selfish person you were before you accepted Christ? Are you a legalistic, cold, doctrinarian Christian; or are you a warm, radiant, loving Christian in whom the world can see Jesus Christ? This is the question for you to ponder.

Make your covenant with Christ today. If you do, you need not fear the judgment, for Christ will be your Advocate and will defend your case in the court of heaven.

B. We are saved by the life and death of Jesus Christ.

If you have accepted the death of Jesus Christ on your behalf, and if you are willing that He impart His perfect character to you, then you are safely protected from God's wrath. You will not be condemned in the judgment. You "shall not come into condemnation." John 5:24. "The Lord will not . . . condemn him when he is judged." Psalm 37:33. "Herein is our love made perfect, that we may have boldness in the day of judgment: because as He is, so are we in this world. There is no fear in love; but perfect love casteth out fear: because fear hath torment. He that feareth is not made perfect in love." 1 John 4:17, 18.

As a born-again Christian you will be considered in the judgment as though you had never sinned. Your character, which you are allowing to be conformed to the image of Jesus, will be made perfect since Christ is imputing His own spotless character to you. You are without spot or wrinkle because you are wearing the white garments of the perfect righteousness of Jesus Christ. Ephesians 5:27.

C. **A new world will dawn.**

Since the time sin entered into our world, every angel and the unfallen beings of other worlds have been eagerly watching developments on this earth. These beings are longing to see the redeemed claim the mansions God has prepared for them in heaven. Romans 8:19. The climax of world history is upon us and will take us suddenly by surprise. Be ready.

This sinful world will soon be utterly destroyed by fire. Sin, Satan, and unrepentant sinners will be destroyed, but the children of God will inherit the new earth. Romans 8:22, 23; 2 Peter 3:10-13.

The Tabernacle of Israel and the Time of Its Cleansing

INTRODUCTION

The tabernacle of Israel and its services shed a great deal of light on the prophecies of Daniel regarding the judgment of believers. Daniel 8:14. The examination of the lives of the believers and the execution of the judgment can be demonstrated from the Bible as clearly as can the teachings of justification, sanctification, and glorification.

"As it is appointed unto men once to die, but after this the judgment." Hebrews 9:27.

"We must all appear before the judgment seat of Christ." 2 Corinthians 5:10.

I. THE SIGNIFICANCE OF THE OLD TESTAMENT TEMPLE SERVICE IN ISRAEL EXPLAINED

A. Here are the chief components of the plan of salvation.

God's plan of salvation has never changed. It has always been the same since the beginning of the world. Believers living in Old Testament times were familiar with the basic tenets of the gospel—the essentials of salvation. Hebrews 4:2, 6.

The Jewish tabernacle in the wilderness and the magnificent temple of Solomon in Jerusalem were symbols of the way God saves man. They were illustrations of the gospel and the plan of salvation.

Before explaining the services that took place in the

tabernacle we will briefly enumerate the chief components of God's plan of salvation.

1. All men are sinners; as a result we are all under the death penalty, called the second death. Romans 5:12.
2. Jesus Christ atoned for the sins of the world once and for all on the cross. No further sacrifice is necessary. Hebrews 10:12.
3. The atonement effected by Christ on the cross for our sins is not automatically applied to us; it must be accepted individually. John 1:12; 3:16.
4. A genuine believer in Christ voluntarily surrenders his life to Him and desires to live forever in intimate union with Jesus through the Holy Spirit. John 15:4; Romans 8:9.
5. Man has a free choice either to accept or to reject God's grace and His commandments. Matthew 16:24.
6. Every individual chooses to serve either Jesus Christ and His principles or Satan and his principles. Luke 11:23; Proverbs 8:36.
7. There is no other way to be saved except through the life, death, and resurrection of Jesus Christ. Acts 4:12.
8. Salvation is offered to us by God as a free gift. It is available to every man through faith. Ephesians 2:8, 9.
9. In order to be saved we must ask God for faith in Him and in His Word. The evidence that we have received faith in Him is our eagerness to obey Him in all things. Hebrews 5:9.
10. All who profess to be believers are being judged by God as to the genuineness of their faith. This judgment decides the fate of every believer, either for eternal life or for eternal death. 2 Corinthians 5:10.
11. Jesus Christ will return to earth a second time as

King of kings and execute the verdict of the judgment. Matthew 25:31, 32.

B. **The gospel is shown in symbols.**

God chose to unfold His plan of salvation gradually. He revealed to Adam through the lamb sacrifices that his sins would only be forgiven by the sacrifice of the Messiah. Abraham was given more light on the gospel when God asked him to sacrifice his own son, who was a symbol of Christ. Then Moses was given the tabernacle and its services which explained the plan of salvation in detail. This progressive revelation culminated in the life of Jesus Christ, His death on the cross, and His resurrection.

The gospel has been the same since the beginning of the world. The basic components have always been the same: one God, one Saviour, the shedding of the blood, acceptance of salvation by faith. The patriarchs, the people of Israel, and Christians have all heard the same gospel. Hebrews 4:2, 6.

Jesus Christ gave Moses the Ten Commandments on Mount Sinai. At the same time He revealed to him the gospel in a clearer form than ever before through the tabernacle and ceremonial laws. Nehemiah 9:12-15; 1 Corinthians 10:4. The tabernacle and the ceremonial laws of Israel were the gospel in shadow form. Israel received a divine visual aid of the gospel. Hebrews 10:1, 8, 9.

When Christ fulfilled God's promises of redemption by laying down His life on the cross for us, the temple and its services and all the ceremonial laws were set aside, for they were no longer needed. The realities had made the symbols obsolete.

C. **The earthly and heavenly tabernacles (sanctuaries) compared.**

The ancient tabernacle of Israel still serves the Christian today for a better understanding of God's plan of salvation.

The book of Hebrews frequently refers to the temple in heaven. Because of the Hebrews' knowledge of the earthly tabernacle services, it was easy for the author of this epistle to enlighten his readers regarding the events taking place in the heavenly temple. The Hebrew Christians were acquainted with the prophecies of Jesus in regard to the destruction of the temple in Jerusalem, which took place in A.D. 70. Because of their Jewish background and tradition they still revered that temple. The author of Hebrews desired to focus their attention away from the earthly temple to the heavenly temple where Jesus Christ was officiating as High Priest and Mediator on behalf of all repentant mankind. Hebrews 6:19, 20.

From the book of Hebrews and the revelation to John we know for certain that there is a magnificent temple in heaven in which Jesus Christ is officiating in our behalf. Revelation 11:19; 15:5. The earthly temple was a small but accurate reproduction of the heavenly temple. Hebrews 8:5.

II. THE EARTHLY SANCTUARY WAS A DWELLING PLACE OF GOD

A. The furniture and compartments of the sanctuary had significance.

1. "Let them make Me a sanctuary; that I may dwell among them." Exodus 25:8. That sanctuary that Moses built had two compartments called the holy place and the most holy place. The sanctuary contained six pieces of furniture: the brazen altar, the water basin, the golden candlestick, the table of shewbread, the altar of incense, and the ark of the covenant which was covered by the mercy seat with its two cherubs. The ark contained the two tables of stone on which God had written the Ten Commandments, the golden pot of manna, and Aaron's rod that had budded.

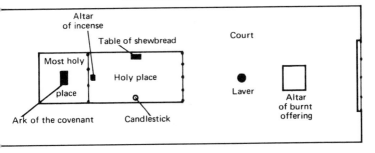

2. Every part of the sanctuary was the gospel in symbols and figures; The sacrificial animals represented Jesus Christ, the Lamb of God. The brazen altar stood for the cross of Christ. The water basin represented the cleansing of the heart from sin. The candlestick symbolized the light of the Holy Spirit. The table of shewbread was a picture of Christ living in the believer. The altar of incense pointed to the worthiness and righteousness of Jesus Christ. The ark of the covenant represented the throne of God from which law and grace flow forth; the throne is also a place of judgment.

   The tabernacle stood for the full gospel message. At no later time did man receive a fuller revelation of God's plan of redemption.

3. The priests who were serving daily in the earthly tabernacle were chosen after the order of Aaron. Jesus Christ, on the other hand, who is serving as High Priest and King in the heavenly sanctuary, was chosen by God after the order of Melchizedek. Hebrews 5:1, 4-6. The order of Aaron was of a temporal nature, while the order of Melchizedek is of an eternal nature.

   The priests and the sacrifices were symbols of the atoning work Jesus Christ was to do for humanity. He was both the sacrificing Priest and the sacrificed Lamb. Hebrews 9:11-14. The priests were

sacrificing animal blood, but Jesus Christ is interceding for us with His own precious blood.

B. **The method used for sacrifice had significance.**

The sinner brought the lamb to the earthly tabernacle to be sacrificed. He laid his hands on the head of
the lamb and confessed his sins, symbolically trans-
mitting his sins to the lamb. The priest then handed him
a knife, with which he killed the lamb. The priest caught
the blood in a vessel, went to the altar, and put
some of the blood on the horns protruding at the four
corners of the altar, thereby symbolically transferring the
sins to the temple. Leviticus 1:4, 5; 4:4-7; 1 John 1:7, 9.

The sins of the believer were forgiven as the lamb
was sacrificed, but his sins were not blotted out until the
yearly Day of Atonement.

C. **The yearly cleansing of the temple, the Day of Atonement, was most solemn.**

Once a year, on the tenth day of the seventh month,
the Day of Atonement, the sins of Israel that had been
transferred to the tabernacle through the lambs that had
been sacrificed throughout the year were removed in an
impressive ceremony.

The description of this ceremony is found in
Leviticus 16. In this ceremony two goats were used, one
standing for Jesus Christ, and the other symbolizing
Azazel or Satan. On this day, the high priest went into
the most holy place with the blood of a special sacrifice,
a goat symbolizing Jesus Christ. He sprinkled the blood
on the mercy seat, over the broken law. Hebrews 9:7.

On this day, the sins of the past year which had been
forgiven were blotted out forever from the temple
record. "For on that day expiation is made for your
cleansing, to cleanse you from all your sins before the
Eternal." Leviticus 16:30, Moffatt. The purpose was "to
abolish sin." Hebrews 9:26, NEB.

Then the high priest left the most holy place and put
the sins of Israel symbolically on the head of a second

goat, which is called the scapegoat. This goat was taken away into the wilderness alive, never to return. Leviticus 16:10, 20-22. The second goat stood for Satan, who will ultimately be made responsible for having caused all our sins. The Day of Atonement, which is called (in Hebrew) Yom Kippur, is looked upon by the Jewish people as a day of judgment.

III. THE EXPLANATION OF THE SYMBOLIC SERVICES IN THE EARTHLY TABERNACLE
A. Daily sacrifices were needed.
When Christians confess their sins they are forgiven through the blood Jesus Christ shed on Calvary. Nevertheless, a record of these sins remains in the books of heaven. Acts 3:19. Their sins are transferred to the temple in heaven, where they remain until the temple is cleansed. The expression, "the cleansing of the sanctuary," refers to the judgment of believers.
B. The Day of Atonement symbolized the judgment of believers.
Before Jesus Christ returns to earth, the record of our sins must be removed from the temple in heaven. The temple will be cleansed of all sins as it was done by the high priest on the Day of Atonement in Israel. Hebrews 9:22, 23. Of course there is no sin in heaven; but there are records of our sins there, and all believers are being judged according to the things which are written in the books. Revelation 20:12. The life record of every man will be weighed in the balance. Romans 2:5-8, 16.

In this judgment, called the investigative judgment, Jesus Christ reveals to all the angels the records of our daily lives. The genuineness of our faith is closely examined. The court wants to know whether the believer had overcome evil by the power of the indwelling Christ. The believer who refuses to accept the power of Jesus Christ to change his character, or the believer who falls away from Christ after having been converted, will be condemned. All sins he committed will be counted against him. Ezekiel 33:12; 2 Peter 2:20, 21. Jesus Christ, rather than being his Advocate, will be his condemning Judge.

If the record of the believer shows that he has claimed victory over his evil nature and has accepted the righteousness of Christ by the power of the indwelling Christ, then the Lord will be his Advocate and intercede for him. He will blot out his sins from the record by His blood, impute His righteousness to him, and leave his name in the book of life. David prayed for this when he said: "Blot out my transgressions." Psalm 51:1.

If you love the Lord Jesus Christ with all your heart, with all your mind, and with all your strength, and desire to obey Him in all things, you need not fear the judgment. You have an Advocate pleading your case before the great grand jury of the universe.

C. **The scapegoat represented Satan.**

We learned that on the Day of Atonement the high priest sacrificed a goat for the sins of Israel which had accumulated during the year; this goat stood for Jesus Christ. Then he placed the sins for which atonement had been made on a second goat, the scapegoat, which symbolized Satan.

When Jesus returns to execute judgment, Satan will be made responsible for being the cause of all sin. During the millennium he and his fallen angels will be the only living beings left in this desolate world. The righteous humans will be in heaven with Jesus, while the unrighteous humans will be dead. Satan, like the scapegoat, will wander aimlessly in his great wilderness, brooding over the senselessness of his rebellion against God. At the end of the millennium, when Christ and the believers return to earth with the Holy City, Satan will be destroyed by fire. Revelation 20:3, 9.

Jesus Christ is the only Sin Bearer of the redeemed.

The goat which symbolizes Azazel, or Satan, is not a sin bearer. After the sins of the redeemed are blotted out from the records of heaven by the blood of Jesus, God will put the blame for having caused them on Satan. He will ultimately be destroyed in the fire of hell. Revelation 20:10, 14.

IV. THE TIME OF THE INVESTIGATIVE JUDGMENT REVEALED

A. The 2,300 years is the longest prophetic time period forecast in the Bible.

The judgment of believers was still future in Jesus' and Paul's day. Matthew 10:15; Acts 24:25; 17:31. It is clear from the Bible that all cases must be settled in God's judgment before Christ's second advent, because His reward for the righteous is with Him. Revelation 22:12.

God had chosen to reveal to man the time of this judgment. Through the prophet Daniel, God gives us the longest time prophecy in the Bible: Daniel 8:13, 14. "Unto two thousand and three hundred days; then shall the sanctuary be cleansed." These 2,300 prophetic days represent calendar years. Ezekiel 4:6; Numbers 14:34. That these days are actually years is also apparent from statements found in Daniel 9, where the period of 490 years allotted to the Jewish nation is apparently to be subtracted from the 2,300-year period. Since the 490 years are to reach to the time of the Messiah, they could not possibly refer to days. Furthermore, Daniel indicates that this longest of Biblical time periods reaches to the time of the end of world history. The vision "relates to the crisis at the close." Daniel 8:17, 19, Moffatt.

Daniel prayed for more understanding of this time period, and God graciously answered his prayer by sending the angel Gabriel with more light on the subject. Daniel 9:21, 22. Following is a diagram of God's schedule of events as revealed to Daniel. Daniel 9:24-27.

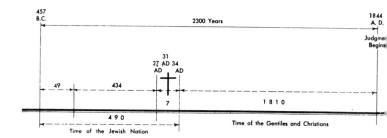

B. **Explanation of the diagram.**

The 2,300 years are broken down into different periods. The first major period covers 70 weeks or 490 years, which is calculated as follows:

$$1 \text{ day } = 1 \text{ year}$$
$$1 \text{ week } = 7 \text{ years}$$
$$70 \text{ weeks } = 490 \text{ years}$$

This period began in the seventh year of King Artaxerxes, or autumn 457 B.C., when the decree was effected that Jerusalem should be restored and rebuilt. Daniel 9:25; Ezra 6:14; 7:7. It ended in A.D. 34.

The 490-year period allotted to the Jewish nation is further divided into three periods:

7 weeks = 49 years, during which Jerusalem was rebuilt.

62 weeks = 434 years, a time of great turmoil.

1 week = 7 years, the ministry of Jesus Christ (3½ years) and the time granted to the Jewish nation to accept the gospel message (another 3½ years).

The prophecy of Daniel stated that in the middle of the last week, or 7 years, the Messiah would be "cut off," or killed, and that all sacrifices would cease. This was fulfilled when Jesus died on the cross in A.D. 31, or 3½ years after He began His ministry. Matthew 27:51.

The second part (3½ years) of the 7 years constituted the last period of grace granted to the Jewish nation as a nation. In A.D. 34 the Jewish Sanhedrin stoned Stephen, the first Christian martyr. With this event the time of grace for the Jewish nation ended, and the gospel was preached to the heathen as well. Acts 8:2, 4; 11:19-21.

The first major time period of 490 years was over. There remained another 1,810 years to make up the full 2,300 years. Counting 1,810 years from the death of Stephen in A.D. 34, we reach A.D. 1844. The prophecy declares: "Then shall the sanctuary be cleansed." Daniel 8:14. This marked the beginning of the investigative judgment in heaven. There was no Jewish sanctuary on earth at that time.

The Bible does not give any time prophecy extending farther than 1844. Christ could have come at any time after this date without violating any prophecy of Scripture. Revelation 10:6.

C. **The time of cleansing of the heavenly sanctuary has arrived.**

A number of prominent Bible students of the past have arrived at the same or a similar interpretation of Daniel 9: Martin Luther, Philip Melanchthon, Nikolaus Selnecker, Georg Nigrinus, Johann Oecolampadius, Heinrich Bullinger, Francisco Rivera, Joseph Mede, William Sherwin, Johanes Cocceius, Johann A. Bengel, Johann P. Petri.

In 1844 Jesus Christ, our great High Priest, began the cleansing of the heavenly sanctuary, or the investigative judgment. Since His ascension Jesus Christ has been interceding for humanity before the throne of God as the only High Priest of mankind; however, since 1844 Christ has been the Advocate in the most holy place of the heavenly temple for all those whose names remain in the book of life. Daniel 7:9, 13.

The apostle John describes the pure church in the

book of Revelation as a pure woman who is clothed with the sun and standing on the moon, symbolizing respectively the New and the Old Testaments. From this we learn that we must consult the whole Bible, both the Old and the New Testaments, in order to arrive at a proper understanding of the teachings of God. We are to find in the whole Bible a beautiful, harmonious pattern. Matthew 13:52.

V. SUMMARY

A. The Jewish passion play of the tabernacle is reenacted by God Himself.

The services in the Jewish tabernacle were a passion play, so to speak, written by God, and pointed ahead to their actual fulfillment. Christ was cast in the chief role. In the place of a brazen altar there was to be a rugged cross, and in the place of an innocent lamb there was to be a sinless Man. The yearly Day of Atonement threw a shadow far into the future, when Jesus Christ would stand before the throne of God and begin the great judgment scene.

The precise structure of the tabernacle, its priests, its ceremonies, its sacrifices, its holy convocations, its yearly cleansing, were meant to instruct the people of God about God's wonderful plan of salvation through Jesus Christ, the Messiah.

In Daniel 12:9, 10 we find that the prophet did not fully understand the meaning of his words. He was told that the full implication of these prophecies would not be known except to the people living in the time of the end of the world. That time is here now and this is why God has shed so much light on the prophecies of Daniel.

The people who understand these events are saying to all men everywhere: "Fear God, and give glory to Him; for the hour of His judgment is come: and worship Him that made heaven, and earth, and the sea, and the fountains of waters." Revelation 14:7.

B. **The judgment is divided into three distinct phases.**
1. The examination of the lives of all believers whose names are written in the book of life. Revelation 20:12.
2. The closing of the time of probation for humanity. The Holy Spirit is withdrawn, and every man is sealed either for eternal life or for eternal death. Revelation 22:11, 12.
3. The execution of the judgment in two parts: the glorification and taking to heaven of the righteous when Christ returns, and the destruction of the unsaved after the millennium in the lake of fire. 1 Thessalonians 4:16, 17; Revelation 20:7, 9, 15.

   There are only two groups of men, the saved and the unsaved. Matthew 25:31-33. Not all who claim to be believers are going to be saved; many among them are unrighteous and will be condemned. 1 Peter 4:17, 18; Luke 13:23-25.

C. **Christ may return in your lifetime.**
   The plan of God is rapidly being fulfilled in all its phases. We are living in the most exciting times of world history. The end of all things is at hand. Few people realize it, and it is hard to draw their attention to the awful events we are about to face.

   Perhaps never before has the world witnessed such a mad worldwide preoccupation with materialism and a selfish pursuit of pleasure, except in the days of Noah. Most people are not prepared to meet Jesus Christ. The majority of Christians are not ready for this great event; they are spiritually asleep. While the courts of heaven are in session and the great grand jury of the universe is judging us, mankind is dancing on its coffin. Nothing can stop God from carrying out His plans as revealed to us through His prophets. Revelation 10:7.

   Is Jesus Christ your Saviour and Lord? Have you humbly received Him as your Redeemer? If not, repent of your sins and receive forgiveness through His blood. Is

Christ dwelling in you? Are you aware of His transforming power in your character? Is He filling your heart with love for your fellowman? If not, repent and ask Jesus to live in you and give you victory over every sinful habit, every temptation, every difficulty. Ask Him to give you His character, His power, because you have a case pending for life or death at the heavenly court. Take now Christ as your Advocate!

Has not Jesus proved that He is a faithful and reliable Saviour? Let us trust, love, and obey Him. "Because thou hast kept the word of My patience, I also will keep thee from the hour of temptation, which shall come upon all the world, to try them that dwell upon the earth." Revelation 3:10.

The Majestic Plan of God for His Redeemed People

INTRODUCTION

The two great opposing forces in this world are Jesus Christ and Satan. Their characters are opposites. On the one hand we have an angel who exalted himself and attempted to become God. On the other we have the eternal Son of God who humbled Himself, became a human being for our sake, and died in a most shameful way on the cross for the sins of the world. He did this to exalt the human race, to lift us up to a place of honor. He realized that "The wages of sin is death." Romans 6:23. But He came to earth saying, "I am come that they might have life." John 10:10.

Since the world began men have either humbled themselves or exalted themselves. Man chooses either one or the other as the basis of his life. "Whosoever exalteth himself shall be abased; and he that humbleth himself shall be exalted." Luke 14:11.

I. GOD IS TURNING REBELS INTO KINGS

A. What was the motive of the first rebellion in heaven?

1. It was strong ambition and self-exaltation that led Lucifer, the highest being ever created by God, into sin and rebellion. In his eagerness to be first in the universe, he attempted to dethrone God and take His place as lord of the universe. "I will exalt my throne above the stars of God." "I will be like the Most High." Isaiah 14:13, 14.

(71)

2. His scheme was bound to fail. The armies of heaven defeated him, and he was banished to this earth. Revelation 12:9. Here he was permitted to continue his warfare against God. He successfully deceived the first pair. Adam and Eve were led to disobey God and rebel against Him. They were prompted by the same spirit of self-exaltation. Satan deceived them through a lie. They were led to believe that if they ate of the fruit of the forbidden tree they would not surely die but would become like gods.

B. **Good counteracts evil.**

1. When Adam and Eve joined Satan in his rebellion, they became God's enemies. Nevertheless, God did not forsake mankind. On the contrary He set into operation the most wonderful plan of salvation to restore the fellowship that had been broken with Him, to unite us more closely with Him than we had ever been before. God's Son became man. He dwelt on this earth in order to seek and to save that which was lost. God's intention was that through Jesus Christ He would make men more precious than the gold of Ophir. He offers us His own righteousness, which makes us perfect as if we had never sinned.

2. Jesus Christ, who has been the instrument of God to fulfill God's plans, is eagerly waiting for the moment when He will be united with us forever in heaven. "Father, I will that they also, whom Thou hast given Me, be with Me where I am." John 17:24. He is waiting for the moment when He can say, "Here am I and the children God has given Me." Hebrews 2:13, Moffatt.

C. **We can be priests and kings of God.**

When Jesus Christ returns to earth in glory, He will take with Him all who by faith in Him have become God's children. When Christ's office of High Priest ceases, the redeemed host of believers will become God's priests and kings in heaven throughout eternity. Revelation 1:6. We marvel at the grace of God: ex-rebels, who have been slaves of Satan, transformed into priests and kings of the mighty God, members of God's family, members of His own household! Ephesians 2:19; 1 John 3:2. Through a miracle of re-creation Jesus Christ has made us forever rebellion-proof, safe and trustworthy. What a magnificent plan God has for us! It is too great for our tiny, narrow minds to grasp; nevertheless, it is true because God has given us His plan in writing. "How unsearchable are His judgments and how inscrutable His ways!" Romans 11:33, RSV.

II. THE UNFOLDING OF GOD'S PLAN OF SALVATION

A. Through grace, sinners become saints.

The repentant sinner who has opened his heart to the wooing of the Holy Spirit and approaches Jesus Christ with a contrite heart, is cleansed by His blood, justified by His righteous life, sanctified by His indwelling Spirit, and finally glorified when Jesus returns.

B. God's testament appoints us His heirs.

God has adopted men as His sons through Jesus Christ. Ephesians 1:5. But He has gone even farther and declared us to be His heirs. "They which are called might receive the promise of eternal inheritance." Hebrews 9:15. The implications of this promise are tremendous. "If children, then heirs; heirs of God, and joint heirs with Christ." Romans 8:17. Wonder of wonders, we have become sons of God; we are allowed to call God our Father; and we are heirs of God and joint heirs with Jesus Christ! Thanks be to God for His inexpressible gift!

C. How large is our inheritance?

God is willing to give everything to His saved children. "He who did not spare His own Son but gave Him up for us all, will He not also give us all things with Him?" Romans 8:32, RSV. Think of all the possessions of God! Imagine the millions of galaxies in His infinite universe. What an indescribably tremendous inheritance!

D. God shares His throne.

God's generosity toward us knows no limits. The Bible contains a promise that is so great that we hardly dare repeat it. God promises believers that He will share His throne with them. This means that they will be permitted to take part in the government of the universe. "To him that overcometh will I grant to sit with Me in my throne." Revelation 3:21.

One can well imagine that other beings in the universe are marveling at this strange promise. They may well ask: How is it possible that ex-rebels shall share the throne of God? Isn't God taking a terrible chance?

This is the crowning act of God's plan of salvation for mankind. He will astonish the whole universe by sharing His throne with human beings, thereby demonstrating once more His unfathomable love and His power to change hearts. God, through Jesus Christ, makes man forever safe from rebellion, forever reliable, forever rebellion-proof. Jesus Christ, by dwelling in us, eliminates every flaw in our character, purges us from every selfish motive, makes us perfect as He is. When He has accomplished this work in us, He will never need to fear that we will turn against Him, or that we will abuse the exalted position He has given us. The Bible gives us the assurance that there will never be another rebellion.

Those that were once as a brand plucked from the fire have now become more precious than the gold of Ophir, and their position is more exalted than if they had never sinned.

E. Behold these exceeding great and precious promises!

Like precious veins of gold, the precious promises of God run through the depths of the Holy Scriptures, filling us with exceeding joy. "That ye may know what is the hope of His calling, and what the riches of the glory of His inheritance in the saints, and what is the exceeding greatness of His power to usward who believe." Ephesians 1:18, 19. Here is another confirmation of this great promise. "And hath raised us up together, and made us sit together in heavenly places in Christ Jesus: that in the ages to come He might show the exceeding riches of His grace in His kindness toward us through Christ Jesus." Ephesians 2:6, 7.

This stupendous plan of God was known in Old Testament times. "He raiseth up the poor out of the dust, and lifteth up the beggar from the dunghill, to set them among princes, and to make them inherit the throne of glory." 1 Samuel 2:8.

III. THE NEW EARTH BECOMES THE CENTER OF THE UNIVERSE

A. God dwells with man.

Hear the precious promises of God for His redeemed! God declares that when the present world of sin and death is no more, the new earth will become the dwelling place of God and man. We will have the indescribable joy of seeing our God face to face. The throne of the universe will be established among men. Revelation 21:22, 23; 22:3, 4.

B. The last shall become first.

The new earth will take the place of the old earth after its destruction. The new earth will become the center of the universe, since God will dwell in it. The place of shame, sin, and death will become a place of glory, righteousness, and life. The new earth will be a lesson to the universe.

God's unfathomable love and wisdom is revealed to man through the Holy Scriptures. All creation is longingly expecting the homecoming of God's redeemed children. What a joy it is to look forward to the fulfillment of these precious promises, to the great event of seeing Jesus Christ face to face. How thrilling to know that we will be permitted to stand before Him and behold His beauty. We know from the prophet Ezekiel that tremendous power issues from the throne of God.

Ezekiel 1. We will be allowed to behold this power without being consumed.

C. **The redeemed host is a sign.**

The redeemed host of mankind will forever be a sign to the whole universe of God's unfathomable love and transcendent power. "When He shall come to be glorified in His saints, and to be admired in all them that believe." 2 Thessalonians 1:10. "Unto me, who am less than the least of all saints, is this grace given, that I should preach among the Gentiles the unsearchable riches of Christ; and to make all men see what is the fellowship of the mystery, which from the beginning of the world hath been hid in God, who created all things by Jesus Christ: to the intent that now unto the principalities and powers in heavenly places might be known by the church the manifold wisdom of God." Ephesians 3:8-10.

D. **Will you be there?**

Return to God your Father as the prodigal son did after he had wasted a good part of his life in the world! How can you resist God's love? Through Jesus Christ He finds what is lost, washes what is impure, covers what in us is unrighteous, raises the dead, makes us again His sons!

> "Love divine, all loves excelling,
> Joy of heaven, to earth come down;
> Fix in us Thy humble dwelling,
> All thy faithful mercies crown!"

> "Jesus, Thou art all compassion,
> Pure, unbounded love Thou art;
> Visit us with Thy salvation,
> Enter every trembling heart."
>
> —Charles Wesley.

"Love knows no limit to its endurance, no end to its trust, no fading of its hope; it can outlast anything." 1 Corinthians 13:7, Phillips.

Let us pray together: Lord Jesus, grant us to be with Thee in Thy eternal kingdom. Amen.

Law, Grace, and the Gospel Are Partners

INTRODUCTION

The law of life is written with indelible letters on every cell, every fiber, and every crystal. These laws regulate life, matter, and energy. Violation of these laws means destruction. The entire universe obeys the will of the Creator. Only man has transgressed the laws of his Creator by sinning. Romans 5:12; 8:20.

Since the fall of man there is an enmity in the human heart against God and His perfect law. Romans 8:7. Since men became sinners, they have been trying to live separate from God and His law. Many suppose that they will never be judged for this attitude and that God has no ground on which to condemn them. This is presumption and deceptive thinking.

I. THE RELATION OF THE MORAL LAW TO THE SINNER

A. What is the moral law? What are the Ten Commandments?

1. The law is the expressed will of God.
2. It is the transcript of His character.
3. It is holy, just and good; it is spiritual. Romans 7:12, 14.
4. It is the everlasting and unchangeable rule for conduct. Psalm 119:89, 152.

B. Sinners find divine help in Jesus Christ.

1. No sinner can keep God's moral law (the Ten Commandments) by his own strength, since through

sin he has become morally too weak. He is ruled by his sinful nature. Only by Jesus Christ living continuously in him can the surrendered believer keep the commandments through the power of the Holy Spirit. Philippians 4:13.

Jesus Christ will not force Himself on the believer; it is a matter of our decision, of our willingness to allow Him to have His way in us. The reception of the life of Jesus Christ in substitution for our own life, and constant surrender to His guidance, is the way of obtaining victory. Galatians 2:20.

2. Some theologians say that Christ has nailed the Ten Commandments to the cross; therefore they do not bind us anymore. See Colossians 2:14. Some men affirm that the newly born Christian is free from the responsibility of keeping the moral law of God since he is under grace. This assertion has no Biblical basis.

In order better to understand this false reasoning, we wish to give an example. Why are men imprisoned? They are in prison because they have broken the law. Having violated these laws, they are "under the law." But if the governor pardons a man, he is no longer "under the law." He is under grace, free from condemnation. Is he therefore free to resume his criminal activities? By no means! He is free to live a law-abiding life.

Christ paid the penalty of the broken law and purchased our pardon. He keeps the law in those who believe in Him and surrender themselves to Him.

II. BOTH LAW AND GRACE ARE NEEDED
A. Why is grace needed for the sinner?

Grace is needed only when a law has been transgressed or when someone has been condemned. If there was no law, there would be no sin. Romans 5:13. If sin does not exist, why do we need grace?

Grace, God's unmerited favor, is moral and spiritual power to lead a new life. 2 Corinthians 12:9. This indwelling divine power is strong enough to enable us to keep His laws. Romans 8:4. God had given mankind a moral law; when man violated it he became too weak to live according to its precepts. God then gave man His grace whereby he could again conform to God's law.

B. Divine grace is needed.

1. Law and grace are precious gifts of God; they are not at war against each other, but rather they are complementary to each other. The grace of God was not given to do away with the law; on the contrary, it was given to fulfill His law. This can be seen from the following words of Paul: "Shall we continue in sin, that grace may abound? God forbid." Romans 6:1, 2. "Shall we sin because we are not under the law, but under grace? God forbid." Romans 6:15.

2. Not to sin means to observe the moral law of God by divine grace. To walk after the Holy Spirit means by the grace of God to live in harmony with the principles of God's law.

    What are these sublime principles? We are to love God and our fellowman. Love toward God is expressed by our keeping of the first four commandments of the Decalogue, while love toward our fellowman is expressed by keeping the last six commandments of the Decalogue. A man who by the grace of God, through the power of the indwelling Christ, lives according to these commandments is free of condemnation. There is harmony and peace in his soul.

3. A Christian does not keep the law in order to earn God's grace and salvation. On the contrary, he keeps the law because he has already received grace. He has been saved by faith in Jesus Christ and by the grace of God has received the power of Jesus Christ in his life to live according to the commandments of God.

He desires to do the whole will of God because he loves Him with all his heart; law and grace are perfectly blended in him. We can truly say that law and grace are partners.

III. BOTH LAW AND THE GOSPEL ARE NEEDED
A. The gospel is God's answer to the demands of the law.
1. What is the relationship between the law and the gospel? The law is the divine standard of righteousness; it is God's requirement for those who wish to live in harmony with Him throughout eternity. Revelation 22:14; Matthew 19:17.
2. After man fell into sin, he became morally weak and unable to keep this divine law in his own strength. He was lost. God in His love and mercy for us devised the plan of salvation. The gospel reveals that plan. The gospel teaches more than forgiveness of sins through Jesus Christ; it also means conversion, the creation of a new man, the giving of divine power to enable this man to conquer his own nature through a power strong enough to overcome sin and temptation. For the first time in his life such a man is empowered to live up to the requirements of God's holy law; this power is the indwelling Christ who lives in him through the Holy Spirit.

B. The plan of creation and the plan of redemption are related.
1. The plan of redemption is auxiliary to the plan of creation. It is easier to create matter than to redeem a people who are lost through sin. Redemption is much more costly to God than creation, since it involves the suffering, the sacrifice, and the death of the Son of God; through Him the whole Godhead suffered. The purpose of the gospel is to restore fallen man to his former state and give him a divine nature that enables him to live according to God's law. The gospel has never done away with this divine

law. This perfect salvation of man was planned by God before the creation of the earth. 1 Peter 1:18-20. Redemption of mankind has never been an afterthought.

2. God's plan of salvation leads the sinner from conversion to justification, to sanctification, and finally to glorification. In a mysterious way God changes the nature of the sinner and turns him into a saint. He becomes righteous by the grace of Jesus Christ. The very nature of Christ becomes ours, and the law of God is perfectly satisfied with the goodness, the righteousness of Jesus Christ, which has become our possession by faith.

C. **Jesus Christ is the Representative of redeemed man.**
　　1. According to the gospel, the Son of God became the Son of Man. He lived in full harmony with God's law, never committing a sin but living a righteous life in a wicked and sinful world. Christ offers His righteous life to every man; He gives it to all who accept Him by faith. He laid down His life for us, taking upon Himself the second death, to rescue man from it. With His blood we are cleansed from all confessed sin.

　　2. Jesus Christ is now our Meditator and High Priest in the heavenly sanctuary. Hebrews 9:24. He is also the Judge of mankind. John 5:22, 27. After the judgment in heaven is finished, Jesus will return the second time and take the righteous to heaven. Hebrews 9:27, 28; 1 Thessalonians 4:16, 17.

D. **The gospel was in effect in Old Testament times.**
　　The gospel was known from the earliest times. Adam, Abel, Seth, Noah, all sacrificed lambs as symbols of the coming "Lamb of God," Jesus Christ. Enoch understood God's plan of redemption and proclaimed the glorious return of the Lord Jesus Christ. Jude 14, 15.

E. **The tabernacle served as a visual aid of the gospel.**

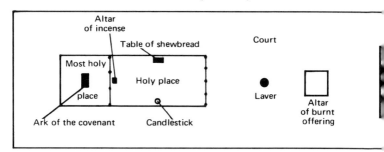

1. The altar of burnt offering symbolized the death of Christ on the cross.
2. The water basin symbolized the new birth and baptism.
3. The candelabra symbolized the light of the Holy Spirit.
4. The table of shewbread symbolized the Lord's life to be lived in us.
5. The altar of incense symbolized Christ's merits, His worthiness, His mediatorial prayers.
6. The ark of the covenant (law and mercy) symbolized the judgment of God.
7. The services in the court stood for the redemption of man.
8. The services in the holy place stood for the sanctification of man.
9. The service in the most holy place stood for the glorification of man.
F. **The ceremonial laws were the gospel in pictures.**
    1. When Moses was in the presence of God on Mount Sinai, he received not only the Ten Commandments but also the gospel in the form of the ceremonial law and the tabernacle services. It was the gospel in shadow form. Exodus 24:12, 18; 25:8, 9. God knew that no man could keep His holy law by his own strength; He provided a way by which He Himself would satisfy its requirements. If man would consent

that God live in him, God Himself would keep His law in the surrendered believer. The ceremonial law, therefore, was a visual demonstration of the plan of salvation. It showed how a sinner could become a saint by the grace of God.

2. As time passed, the purpose of the tabernacle services and the meaning of the ceremonial laws were lost by Israel. They could no longer understand their deep significance: the redemption and sanctification of both body and soul. In the years that followed, both priests and people repeated daily the requirements of the ceremonial laws without realizing their implication. When Jesus Christ, God incarnate, came to earth to become the reality of the gospel, to fulfill all the symbols (Colossians 2:14), Israel refused to understand. It did not recognize Him.

IV. EVERY MAN NEEDS GOD'S LAW, HIS GRACE, AND HIS GOSPEL

A. If there is no law, the mercy of God and the gospel are not needed.

If God had provided a moral law without offering us grace and the gospel, humanity would be lost. No sinner could fulfill the requirements of God's law by his own strength. If this had been God's plan, God could be called righteous, but He could not be called merciful.

The law can only show us the rules of righteousness to give us a picture of a model character, but it cannot cleanse the sinner or give him strength to keep the law.

B. Jesus Christ is the embodiment of the gospel.

Salvation can only be accomplished by one who is more powerful than the law, namely God Himself. He paid the price of sin. He is willing to live, through His Holy Spirit, in every surrendered man in helping him to live up to every moral requirement of the law. In the judgment Jesus Christ imputes to every saved man His matchless life, His own righteousness.

C. **Love is the basis of the law and the gospel.**
1. The grace of God and the gospel have no purpose if there is no law and no condemnation. Romans 4:15. For this reason law and grace balance each other. Both have the same basis: the love of God. Both have the same goal: the salvation of man.
2. God is love. 1 John 4:16.
   a. God's law is love. Romans 13:10; Matthew 22:37-40.
   b. Grace is love. Ephesians 2:8; John 3:16.
   c. The gospel is love. Ephesians 3:19.
   d. At the cross of Calvary law and grace were perfectly blended. Psalm 85:10. "Mercy and truth are met together."
   e. By divine charter, God's law, grace, and gospel have been partners from the beginning of human history. No man can divorce them.

Christ's Relationship to the Moral Law and to Good Works

INTRODUCTION

One often hears in Christian circles that a man is saved by faith alone, irrespective of his observance of the moral law and his performance of good works. Let us study the Scripture and see what Jesus taught on the relationship between faith and obedience, faith and works.

I. MAN IS CREATED A MORAL BEING, GOVERNED BY MORAL LAWS

A. Jesus Christ is the Creator of the universe.

1. Laws are necessary in creation. They control all matter and all living beings. The Son of God is the great Lawgiver. Christ wrote His law in the human mind when He created us. The Christ of the New Testament is the Jehovah of the Old Testament. No man has ever seen God the Father. John 1:18.

2. It was Jesus Christ who gave Israel, through Moses on Mount Sinai, the Ten Commandments. Nehemiah 9:10-13; 1 Corinthians 10:4. Jesus Christ gave a detailed explanation of the deep implications of the Ten Commandments in His sermon on the mount of blessings. Matthew 5:17, 18, 21, 22, 27, 28, 31, 32, 38, 39. He showed His hearers the spirituality of the law and taught them that these principles affected every aspect of their lives.

B. **Jesus Christ magnified His moral law.**

    1. Man sinned by transgressing the law of God. 1 John 3:4. The Redeemer of the human race began His work of redemption at the place where the first Adam failed. Adam failed to keep the moral law of God; he was disobedient. Had Jesus, during His lifetime, transgressed the least of these commandments only once, He would have sinned and lost the battle with Satan. "Which of you convinceth Me of sin?" John 8:46. "I delight to do Thy will, O My God; yea, Thy law is within My heart." Psalm 40:8.

    2. It was prophesied that the Messiah would magnify and glorify the law of God. Isaiah 42:21. Jesus fulfilled this prophecy. Matthew 5:17, 18.

C. **Mount Sinai and Golgotha are not rivals.**

    1. The significance of the events which occurred on Mount Sinai and Golgotha are complementary and not contradictory to one another. On Mount Sinai Christ demanded that His people obey Him, while through His life and death He made it possible for man to obey these precepts. Christ Himself keeps His holy law in us.

    2. The law demanded two things from the Redeemer; first, that He lead a totally sinless life, and second, that He pay the penalty for man's transgression. Jesus did both. On the cross He paid the penalty for us, the second death.

        Only sinless, just men are allowed to live forever. The righteous life of Jesus Christ is imputed and imparted freely to the believer. It is a great pity that so few avail themselves of this gift.

    3. Satan has had great success in putting Jesus Christ and the moral law, Golgotha and Mount Sinai, into opposition to one another as if they were enemies. Jews say that they have nothing to do with Golgotha and Jesus Christ, and many Christians claim that they have nothing to do with Mount Sinai and the

law. Millions of religious people believe this lie. Satan successfully deceived the Jews and made them think that Jesus was against the law and the temple; similarly, he is deceiving the Christian world with the assertion that the moral law and good works are not part of Jesus Christ and His faith.

D. **Jesus honored the moral law.**

1. Jesus Christ honored and kept His own laws. John 15:10. "He that hath My commandments, and keepeth them, he it is that loveth Me." John 14:21. When Jesus gave His disciples what He called a "new" commandment, "Love one another; as I have loved you" (John 13:34), He merely stressed the second great commandment, "Thou shalt love thy neighbor as thyself." Matthew 22:39.

2. The New Testament stands on the same foundation as the Old Testament, namely, the moral law of God. In Old Testament times as well as now believers were keeping the moral law by the indwelling Spirit of God; both in Old Testament and in New Testament times some men have attempted to keep the moral law through their own strength. This is impossible. They are rightly called "legalists."

   At the creation Christ wrote the moral law in man's heart and mind. Christ does the same today with a man who gives himself to Him. Hebrews 8:10.

3. Christ will be the Judge. John 5:22, 27. The basis of judgment will be His holy law. James 1:23-25; 2:10.

4. The distinguishing marks of God's people living at the end of world history are clearly given in Revelation 14:12: "Here are they that keep the commandments of God, and the faith of Jesus." This points out that it is not only a faith *in Jesus* that we need, but the faith *of Jesus*; the very faith that Jesus had when He was on earth can be ours too.

   Who will enter the New Jerusalem? The answer is found in Revelation 22:14: "Blessed are they that do His commandments, that they may have right to the tree of life, and may enter in through the gates into the city." But the believers who delight in keeping the commandments of God are the very ones chosen by Satan for his most vicious attacks. Revelation 12:17.

E. **The moral law of God is still in force.**

1. If there is no law, then there is no sin and therefore no necessity of redemption. Only the law shows us what sin is. Romans 3:20. The law cannot cleanse us from our sinful natures; it cannot forgive our sins. And it gives us no strength to keep from falling into sin. The law sends us to Jesus Christ who alone cleanses us from our sinful natures, forgives our sins, and provides the power to cease sinning. The law is a tutor leading sinners to Jesus Christ. Galatians 3:24.

2. The Jewish people also received the gospel, but only in symbols, in visual aids—through the ceremonial laws, the temple services, and the annual feasts. These three represented the gospel until the reality, Jesus Christ, came into the world. Hebrews 4:2, 6. In all of these symbols they were to see Jesus Christ, the Messiah. He is our High Priest, the sacrificial Lamb, the Mediator, the Advocate, and the Judge. Christ fulfilled every aspect of the ceremonial laws; these ceremonies have ceased because Jesus Christ, the Reality, has come. Daniel 9:27; Matthew 27:51; Colossians 2:14; Hebrews 10:1, 14.

3. The moral law, the Ten Commandments, is still in operation and is performing its appointed duty: It points out sin and causes us to take refuge in Christ. Since the death of Jesus Christ, sinners do not go through the ceremonies of the ceremonial law, but they go to Christ Himself to find redemption. He is the solution of our problem of sin.

4. Jesus Christ is the embodiment of the moral law. The promised Saviour, the plan of salvation, the way

of justification, sanctification, and glorification of the repentent sinner were all revealed in the types and shadows of the ceremonial law and in the temple services. These were an answer to the moral law and made it glorious.

5. The keeping of the moral law, the performance of good works, can never save a soul. On the other hand, the continuous refusal to obey the smallest commandment of God or the lack of good works in the life of a believer shuts him out of heaven, for it demonstrates that Christ is not living in him. Matthew 25:29, 30. James 2:17, 18.

II. THE RELATIONSHIP BETWEEN THE FAITH OF JESUS AND GOOD WORKS

A. Faith is necessary.

1. All the gracious gifts of God become ours through faith. "Without faith it is impossible to please Him." Hebrews 11:6.

2. The Holy Spirit dwells in us through faith. Romans 1:17; Ephesians 3:17. Christ's virtues, His strength, and His character become ours by faith. Romans 3:28. Faith supports the moral law. Romans 3:27, 31.

3. Both law and faith have their particular functions. "This is the victory that overcometh the world, even our faith." 1 John 5:4.

B. What are the effects of our faith?

1. Faith is neither the ground nor the end of our salvation; it is only the seeing eye, the hearing ear, the grasping hand. It is only the means to make Jesus Christ and His redemption personal. Faith is a trust in God that He will do what He has promised. It is because we trust in Him that we act according to our faith and live according to His commandments.

2. It is by faith that we accept Jesus Christ as our personal Lord and Saviour. Acts 2:36, 41. Many are

willing to receive Him as their Saviour but not as their Lord. It is not enough to believe the theory of truth. We must also live by His grace according to His truth. All men will be judged by their deeds. Revelation 22:12.

3. The form of Christianity which does not require from the believer a struggle with his old sinful nature and does not demand self-denial and the hatred of every form of sin is a counterfeit Christianity. Unfortunately this kind is very popular today. True faith in Christ means a constant fight for His principles. "Fight the good fight of faith." 1 Timothy 6:12.

4. To have a true faith in Christ means to accept the benefits of the gospel as well as its obligations. Faith and surrender to Christ do not mean inactivity in our spiritual lives; they denote full cooperation with God and the Holy Spirit in overcoming our sinful tendencies. We must employ every power and ability supplied to us by the indwelling Christ to do the will of God and serve Him. The Bible promises condemnation to those who do not have a practical Christianity. Matthew 25:41-46.

C. **Faith without works is dead.**

1. True and living faith is manifested by good deeds, "faith which worketh by love." Galatians 5:6.

The right relationship between faith and good works is described in James 2:14, 17, 18, 21, 24.

What importance did Jesus Christ ascribe to good works? The answer is found in Matthew 7:21: "Not everyone that saith unto Me, Lord, Lord, shall enter into the kingdom of heaven; but he that doeth the will of My Father." In 1 John 2:4 we read, "He that saith, I know Him, and keepeth not His commandments, is a liar." And in Luke 6:46 Jesus says, "Why call ye Me, Lord, Lord, and do not the things which I say?"

2. Noah believed in the coming Flood and built an ark. Hebrews 11:7. Abraham believed that God could raise Isaac from the dead and was willing to offer his son as a sacrifice. Hebrews 11:17-19; James 2:23, 21, 22. In the same way, God's people living at the time of the return of Christ will have both: the faith of Jesus and obedience to His commandments. Revelation 14:12.

III. THERE IS WONDERFUL HARMONY IN THE NEW LIFE IN CHRIST

A. The faith of Jesus brings forth good works.

There is a wonderful harmony between our faith in Jesus, the keeping of the commandments of God, and good works. They blend together beautifully. Each one does its divinely appointed task.

Divine faith is a gift of God offered to every man, but few wish to receive it. God gives the believer divine power and grace to do deeds of love and to obey His commandments. Through faith in Jesus Christ we are continually connected with God. "Who are kept by the power of God through faith unto salvation." 1 Peter 1:5.

B. Lack of love and a lack of will to do good deeds demonstrate a dead faith.

1. A man can say he believes in Jesus Christ as his Saviour, that he believes in all His teachings and promises, but his faith is dead and does not lead to salvation if he fails to put his faith into action in his daily life.

2. A man can have great faith and strong convictions; yet if he is without love which is expressed in noble and selfless good works in the service of God and humanity, his faith is worthless. 1 Corinthians 13:2.

3. No man is justified or saved by the moral law or by good works; to believe this is a heathen concept of salvation. Unfortunately, this idea had captured the minds of the Jewish people at the time of Christ and

led them to total spiritual ruin. It has also contaminated the faith of many Christians.

We are justified only by faith in Jesus Christ, by relying on His righteousness. This living faith is bound to express itself in daily deeds, which in turn molds our characters according to the divine image. Such a living faith cannot be hidden; it shines like a burning lamp. It radiates warmth to all those living around us.

4. The genuineness of our faith when tested brings forth good fruit because we love God. By faith we are more than conquerers.

Israel Opposes the Gospel, and Christendom Opposes the Moral Law

INTRODUCTION

One of the great tragedies in the history of the world is that few men have had a clear understanding of the plans and purposes of God. The grace which God poured out upon all mankind has always been greatly misunderstood. As a result, man's reasoning has been in collision with God's plans. Since Adam, man has been at enmity with God and has, consciously or unconsciously, been fighting Him. This has been true not only of the heathen world but also of God's chosen nation, Israel, as well. "The ox knoweth his owner, and the ass his master's crib: but Israel doth not know, My people doth not consider." Isaiah 1:3.

I. THE LAW AND THE GOSPEL HAVE BEEN PARTNERS SINCE THE BEGINNING

A. Man's reaction to God's plan.

1. The plan of redemption was not an afterthought of God; it was planned before creation began. "Christ was foreordained before the foundation of the world." 1 Peter 1:20. As soon as sin entered the human mind, the grace of God became effective. "I will put enmity between thee and the woman." Genesis 3:15.

2. Proud men accepted the law of God, but because of self-righteousness many rejected the gospel of grace. They wanted to be righteous by their own efforts.

(93)

This has been the attitude of most religious people throughout history.

B. **Messengers of God's plan.**

1. Noah was a preacher of righteousness, and his message was the gospel. His ark was a symbol of grace and redemption. Noah and his message were ridiculed and rejected.

2. Abraham, Isaac, and Jacob were messengers of God's plan of salvation. They spoke of the coming of the Messiah. Daily they offered animal sacrifices, demonstrating their faith in the coming Messiah. However, only a few of their contemporaries accepted this concept of redemption; instead they sacrificed animals, children, and sometimes themselves to their idols.

II. ISRAEL STRUGGLED AGAINST THE GOSPEL

A. **The moral law versus the ceremonial law.**

God gave Israel the moral law and the gospel through Moses on Mount Sinai. The moral law was given to them on two tables of stone. The first four commandments represent our love toward God, and the other six represent our love toward man. See Exodus 20:2-17.

The gospel, which is God's plan of salvation for man, was given to Moses through the ceremonial law, the tabernacle and its priestly services, and the annual feasts. These institutions prefigured the coming of the Redeemer; they were symbols of God's plan of salvation from Eden lost to Eden restored. "Those who formerly received the good news failed to enter." Hebrews 4:6, RSV.

B. **The purpose of the sacrificial services.**

The temple services, the daily sacrifices, and the annual feasts lost their meaning through formalism; they became the aim rather than the means. The sacrifices in the temple became an empty ceremony. The average person believed that he was paying for his sins by bringing a lamb to the priest, and that by so doing he was earning salvation. The beautiful gospel, foreshadowed in these symbolic services which prefigured the redemptive work of the Messiah, was misinterpreted. The ceremonies became the tool of self-righteousness, formalism, and legalism. Their wrong attitude can be read in these words: "All that the Lord has spoken we will do." Exodus 19:5, 8. Israel became proud of its temple. Jeremiah 7:3, 4. Israel offered God its own righteousness. Romans 9:30-32; 10:2, 3. This was the spiritual climate at the time when Jesus began His ministry.

C. **The services in the tabernacle pointed to Christ and to His mission.**

    1.   *a.* The altar typified the cross of Calvary.

          b. The water basin typified the cleansing we receive.

          c. The candelabra signified the Holy Spirit.

          d. The shewbread typified the Lord's life lived in us.

          e. The altar of incense foreshadowed the mediation and merits of Christ.

          f. The ark signified the throne of God; God's judgment.

    2. Jesus Christ was symbolized by the lamb that was sacrificed, by the high priest, by the shewbread, and by the incense offered.

    3. God's plan of salvation was also prefigured in the annual feasts and sabbaths. Leviticus 23. The first four celebrations took place in the spring. They stood for events that took place at the time of Christ's first coming.

          a. The slaying of the Passover lamb stood for the death of Jesus Christ. 1 Corinthians 5:7.

          b. The Feast of Unleavened Bread symbolized cleansing from sin. 1 Corinthians 5:7, 8.

          c. The waving of the sheaf, or firstfruits, signified the resurrection of Jesus Christ. 1 Corinthians 15:20, 23.

    d. Pentecost, the Feast of Weeks, prefigured the outpouring of the Holy Spirit.

        The next three celebrations were in the autumn and stood for events taking place at the time of Christ's second coming.

    e. The New Year, the blowing of trumpets, symbolized the message to be given the world before the antitypical day of atonement.

    f. The Day of Atonement symbolized the time of judgment, the application of the righteousness of Christ to the lives of all who believe in Jesus.

    g. The Feast of Tabernacles, or ingathering, was a symbol of the ingathering of God's people in the new earth, Eden restored.

D. Symbols are replaced by realities.

The symbols described above were shadows pointing to Jesus Christ and His mission. They were fulfilled and abolished by Him. Hebrews 9:11, 12, 23, 24; 10:1, 2, 8, 9, 14. Daniel prophesied that these symbols would be fulfilled. Daniel 9:27. Paul stated that the method of offering sacrifices under the ceremonial laws was nailed to the cross. Colossians 2:14.

As soon as the reality comes, symbols and shadows cease to be observed; in the same way we do not depend on a man's picture for a description when we meet him personally. Unfortunately, the rabbis and scribes refused to grasp the true meaning of the symbols. The whole emphasis was given to the symbols themselves; they became an end rather than a means. The ceremonial activities became the national and religious pride. They refused to give them up after Jesus fulfilled them. They missed the point of them.

E. Jesus clashed with the rabbis.

    1. The rabbis and scribes soon noticed that Jesus avoided them. He never brought sacrifices to the temple.

    2. Jesus tried to convince them that He was the

fulfillment of these ceremonies. He said to them, "In this place is One greater than the temple." Matthew 12:6. And, "Before Abraham was, I Am." John 8:58.

3. Jesus associated Himself with common people and sinners. Mark 2:16.

4. Jesus said, "Come unto Me, all ye that labor and are heavy-laden." Matthew 11:28. He did not ask any authority from the priesthood. Matthew 21:23.

5. Jesus called sinners to repentance and forgave their sins, without sending them first to the temple to sacrifice lambs. Mark 2:17, 5.

6. The priests became envious of Him, since the people listened to His teachings and praised Him for His miracles of healing.

7. Jesus showed His contempt for their hypocrisy. He rebuked them for their greed and selfishness, for placing the emphasis on the outward appearance while leaving the soul unreformed and untouched. He told them that this same spirit had led men in the past to kill the prophets who had called for spiritual revivals and for a change in their lives.

8. Jesus put the emphasis on the power of God which alone can change the sinner and make him a saint. The priests and philosophers, on the other hand, put the emphasis on the ceremonies and relied on good deeds for this change in character.

9. Jesus said, "Repent ye, and believe the gospel." Mark 1:15. The rabbis, on the other hand, referred to the fathers and to the traditions which Jesus rejected. Matthew 15:2, 7-9.

10. They accused Jesus of deceiving and misleading the people with false teachings. He was called an agent of the devil, healing by the power of Satan. They called Him a false Messiah because He had social relationships with sinners and did not promote the political greatness of the Jewish nation.

F. Sad results followed this attitude.

The gospel was a stumbling block to the Jews. When Jesus raised up Lazarus, they decided to kill Him. John 11:46, 47, 50. When Jesus claimed to be the Son of God, they planned His immediate death. Mark 14:61-64. The priests and rabbis rejected the gospel of Christ because they refused to give up their loyalty to the ceremonial laws and their spirit of nationalism; they did not recognize the intimate relationship between the gospel and the ceremonial laws.

It is indeed a strange phenomenon that after the Jewish nation had waited 1,500 years for their Messiah and had practiced the symbolism of the gospel through their daily and yearly temple services and feasts, the Jewish leaders and the nation rejected both their Messiah and His gospel.

III. CHRISTIANS STRUGGLE AGAINST THE MORAL LAW OF GOD

The same spirit of antagonism described above has been prevalent among many Christians. These Christians are not fighting the gospel, but are opposing the moral law; they have, indeed, rejected it. In the beginning Christians proclaimed the full gospel of Jesus Christ to all the world; but soon extremism began, and the fight against the Ten Commandments of God was on.

A. Grace is not a license to sin.

In the eighteenth century, just before the time of Wesley, antinomian teachings brought a spiritual decline in England. It was taught then that Christ had abolished the moral law and that Christians were free from this bondage. It was said that divine grace superseded the keeping of the Ten Commandments. Today some Christians even believe that the violation of the moral law by a born-again person is not regarded by God as a transgression; they claim that at conversion the blood of Christ cleansed the believer forever from all sins committed in the past or to be committed in the future, regardless of whether he repents of them and confesses them.

This has led some Christians to think that over-coming evil character traits (irritability, self-indulgence, prejudice, et cetera) by the power of the indwelling Christ is optional; they do not think they can ever lose salvation regardless of how they live. Theirs is a false reasoning.

These teachings are antichristian and emanate from the lawless one. This teaching is based on the premise that there is no unchangeable law of God. This leads to the thinking that the standard of morality is always determined by society, and that the standard changes with time and customs.

B. **The gospel is complementary to the law of God.**

Wesley opposed these teachings, since they are contrary to the Holy Scriptures. He stated that Christ came not to abolish the moral law but to fulfill and to magnify it. Matthew 5:17, 18.

The law and the gospel are in perfect harmony; they blend with and point to one another. The truth of the matter is that the power of God's grace is given us so that the righteousness of the law might be fulfilled in us through the Spirit of the indwelling Christ. Romans 8:4.

How is it possible to honor Jesus Christ when we overthrow His law and destroy His teachings? If we do away with His law, there is no necessity for the preaching of the gospel, because where there is no law, there is no sin. Romans 5:13; 1 John 3:4. Only the law tells us that we are sinners. Romans 3:20.

Paul exposed two major errors prevalent in his time:

1. The error of thinking that the ceremonial laws were still in force and must be observed by Christians.

2. The error of thinking that man can earn salvation by keeping the law of God.

   Both errors are unscriptural and are characteristic of legalism. On the other hand, Paul upheld the teaching that the moral law is kept by the believer through the indwelling Christ. Hebrews 8:10; Philippians 4:13; Romans 8:4. As long as Christ lives in the heart of the believer, His divine law is engraved upon it.

Paul makes clear in Galatians 5 and 6 that a man who has already found justification in Christ will live by the law of Christ. He will faithfully comply with all that Christ requires of him, not as a means of salvation, but because of his whole-souled love for Christ. Then, and only then, will the glorious fruit of the Spirit reach maturity in his life.

C. **Who promotes this teaching of lawlessness? Who is the one who began this movement against the moral law of God?**

1. "And he shall speak great words against the Most High, and shall wear out the saints of the Most High, and think to change times and laws." Daniel 7:25.

2. "For the mystery of lawlessness is already at work." "The lawless one will be revealed." 2 Thessalonians 2:7, 8, RSV.

3. Just before Christ's return Satan will fight against those who keep the commandments of God. Revelation 12:17.

D. **The controversy recurs.**

We hear from Christian pulpits today that Christ has nailed the moral law to the cross, that He has fulfilled it for us, that we are under grace and not under law; sometimes we even hear it said that a man is saved no matter how he lives. These sincere people are fighting against the moral law of God with the same spirit and fervency as Israel fought against the gospel of Jesus Christ.

A person who still believes that the law of God is eternal and that it can be fulfilled by the in-dwelling Christ is often wrongly called a legalist today. The fact remains, however, that the grace of

Jesus Christ is sufficient to enable us to obey all of His commandments.

"If ye keep My commandments, ye shall abide in My love." John 15:10.

"Shall we continue in sin, that grace may abound? God forbid." "Shall we sin because we are not under the law, but under grace? God forbid." Romans 6:1, 2, 15.

E. **Satan is the enemy of the law and the gospel.**

It is interesting that as we are nearing the end of the world, the old controversy is flaring up again. Satan is the archenemy of both the gospel and the moral law, since Christ is the Author of both.

Satan prompted the Jewish leaders and their nation to oppose the gospel of Jesus Christ, while today he inspires well-meaning Christians to oppose the moral law of God and to persecute those who by the grace of God wish to keep it.

This is the modern version of Satan's old enmity against Jesus Christ, against His moral law, against His plan of salvation, against His gospel, and against those who wish to live by His indwelling Spirit. Everyone today has to decide where he stands in this controversy. "Open Thou mine eyes, that I may behold wondrous things out of Thy law." Psalm 119:18.

"I am not ashamed of the gospel of Christ: for it is the power of God unto salvation." Romans 1:16.

"Here are they that keep the commandments of God, and the faith of Jesus." Revelation 14:12.

Christ Is in the Sabbath

INTRODUCTION

According to Genesis 1:26 God is our Creator; more specifically, it is the Son of God, Jesus Christ, who is the Creator of all things in cooperation with the Father. Colossians 1:15-17. Jesus is the Upholder of all things in this universe. Hebrews 1:1-3.

I. **JESUS IS THE SAME IN THE OLD TESTAMENT AS IN THE NEW TESTAMENT**
    A. **The Son of God is the Lawgiver and the Redeemer. Isaiah 33:22; 1 Corinthians 10:4.**
        1. It was Jesus Christ who gave Moses the Ten Commandments on Mount Sinai. See James 4:12. Later, in His Sermon on the Mount, Jesus interpreted the deeper meaning of the Ten Commandments and their practical application. Matthew 5, 6, and 7.
        2. No mortal has ever seen God the Father. John 1:18.
        3. Christ as Yahweh, or Jehovah, is the One who led Israel out of Egypt to the land of Canaan. It was Christ who was in the pillar of fire and in the cloud, leading Israel through the Red Sea and the wilderness. Christ was the Rock. 1 Corinthians 10:1-9. Again, it was Christ who supplied Israel with the manna in the wilderness. John 6:32. Moses wrote of Him. John 5:46.

4. Abraham and other Bible prophets foresaw Christ as the coming Redeemer. John 8:56, 58.

B. **Christ is the Lord of the Sabbath.**

The same divine Person who led Israel in Old Testament times is the One who has been leading the spiritual Israel of the New Testament.

1. It was God's Son, the preexistent Christ, who established the seventh-day Sabbath. Genesis 2:1-3.

2. The objects or aims of the Sabbath day were: a remembrance and an acknowledgment of His creation, a seal of God's people, a protection from false beliefs, and a way of intimate communion with God.

3. From its inception, therefore, the Sabbath day has been a Christian institution, since it was given by Christ before the fall of man. The Sabbath, therefore, is not a Jewish holiday, but is given to all believers in Christ. When Adam and Eve were driven out of the Garden of Eden because of their rebellion against God, they took with them two institutions that Christ had given them: the institution of marriage, and the seventh-day Sabbath. The Bible states that the Sabbath was made for *man*. Mark 2:27, 28. Nowhere does the Bible say it was made for the Jewish race only.

4. The Person who led Israel out of Egypt is the One who gave them the Sabbath rest—Jesus Christ.

C. **The seal of God.**

1. The Sabbath rest is an everlasting sign and seal between God and His redeemed people. Exodus 31:14, 17.

   The three components of a seal are the name (*e.g.,* George Washington); the position (*e.g.,* President); and the area of his authority (*e.g.,* U.S.A.). The same terminology applies to God's seal as expressed in the fourth commandment in Exodus 20:11: name, God; position, Creator; area of authority, heaven and earth.

2. In the last days God's people will be sealed. Revelation 7:2, 3. This seal refers to a state of mind. They "remember" God's day.

II. THE SABBATH WAS GIVEN TO MANKIND FOR ALL AGES

A. Men had knowledge of the true Sabbath before Sinai.

1. It was given to Adam and to his posterity. Genesis 2:1-3; Mark 2:27.
2. The manna was given to Israel in the wilderness before they received the Ten Commandments on Mount Sinai. Exodus 16:22-30. It fell on the first six days of the week but not on the seventh, Sabbath.

B. The Sabbath is an institution for all men.

The Ten Commandments were given on Mount Sinai. Exodus 20:3-17.

1. The Sabbath is a sign between God and His people. Exodus 31:13, 17.
2. The Sabbath was intended for the Gentiles too. Isaiah 56:6, 7.
3. The Scriptures foretold that the coming Messiah would magnify the Sabbath. Isaiah 42:21.
4. Like all of the other commandments of God, the fourth commandment was kept by Jesus. Psalm 40:7, 8.
5. The Sabbath will be restored and will be kept at the end of world history, just before the

return of the Lord Jesus Christ. Isaiah 58:12-14; Revelation 12:17.

C. **The Bible makes a distinction between the weekly Sabbath and the yearly sabbaths.**

1. This was exemplified during the Jewish economy.
    a. The weekly, recurring seventh-day Sabbath God calls "The Sabbath of the Lord." Exodus 20:10; Leviticus 23:3, 38.
    b. Concerning the yearly sabbaths, the Bible calls each "a sabbath." Leviticus 23:24, 32.
2. The weekly Sabbath day observance is entirely different from all the other feasts and holy convocations. It is not peculiar to the Jewish nation because it originated at creation. (See Leviticus 23:3, 4, 37, 38. And note the phrase, "*besides* the Sabbaths of the Lord.")
3. The weekly Sabbath of the Lord belongs to mankind. It "was made for man." Mark 2:27. That was the reason the Sabbath was incorporated in the Ten Commandments. It existed before sin entered into the world, and it will exist when there is no sin and no sinner. Isaiah 66:22,23.
4. The annual feasts had sabbaths that were made for Jews and that foreshadowed the plan of salvation through Jesus Christ. Hebrews 10:1. These were the following: (1) two sabbaths for the Passover and for the Feast of Unleavened Bread; (2) the sabbath of Pentecost; the sabbath of the Feast of Trumpets; the sabbath of the Day of Atonement; and two sabbaths of the Feast of Tabernacles.
5. Many Christian Jews in Jerusalem and in the Roman Empire at the time of Paul still observed these "shadow sabbaths," which were foreshadowing Christ, the reality. The ceremonial sabbaths were shadows cast by the heavenly realities. Paul definitely knew the distinction made by Moses between the two kinds of sabbaths. Leviticus 23:37, 38.

(Please note the word "besides.") The apostle Paul warned the Christian Jews not to lay any importance on the shadow or ceremonial sabbaths. Galatians 4:10; Colossians 2:16, 17.

When Jesus Christ died on the cross, these shadow, ceremonial sabbaths were fulfilled and had no binding effect whatsoever on Christians. The weekly "Lord's Sabbath," on the other hand, is in contrast to the shadowy sabbath. That Lord is none other than Jesus Christ, the Creator, who instituted it and called it "My holy day."

6. Israel and Judah rarely kept the Sabbath of the Lord in the correct manner. Their unfaithfulness in this was one of the reasons for the Babylonian captivity. Jeremiah 17:22, 27.

III. JESUS CHRIST AND HIS APOSTLES KEPT THE SABBATH

A. Jesus set the example in Sabbath keeping.

1. Jesus regularly went to the synagogue on the Sabbath day. Luke 4:16; Matthew 13:54; Mark 1:21, 22.

2. The collisions with the Pharisees were never caused over the question of which day was the Sabbath, but over the *manner* of observance of this day. Jesus risked His life several times to show the people the true meaning of Sabbath keeping. He desired to correct their erroneous traditions.

3. When Jesus died, His disciples honored His custom of Sabbath rest by burying Him before the Sabbath began at sundown Friday. He remained in His tomb over the Sabbath hours while His disciples rested "according to the commandment." It was no accident that He died late Friday afternoon and rose early the following Sunday morning. Luke 23:52 to 24:3.

B. The disciples follow Christ's example.

1. The disciples observed the Sabbath day too. Luke 23:54-56.
2. Jesus Christ gave instructions to the Christians to keep the Sabbath forty years later. In A.D. 31 He spoke of Sabbath keeping in A.D. 70, at which time the destruction of Jerusalem took place. Matthew 24:20.
3. Paul kept the Sabbath with Jews and Gentiles. Acts 16:12, 13; 17:1, 2; 18:4, 11; 13:42; 1 Corinthians 7:19.

IV. THE GOSPEL MESSAGE IS IN THE SABBATH

A. The Sabbath is a sign of the true rest to be found in Christ.

1. Jesus said, "Come unto Me, . . . and I will give you rest." Matthew 11:28.
2. When we observe the Sabbath in the right spirit, there is rest for the body and for the soul, foreshadowing our rest in heaven. Hebrews 4:7-10. Resting on the Sabbath, we look forward to our complete redemption when we will rest in heaven, free from the presence of sin. The Sabbath rest which we observe every week honors a commandment which we keep out of love for our Saviour. It is a type of the rest we will enjoy with Him in heaven. The Jewish people did enter the land of Canaan under Joshua, but did not enter into the soul rest of the Redeemer.
3. The Sabbath is a promise of:
   a. The inheritance of the new earth.
   b. The transformation of character into the likeness of Jesus Christ which qualifies us to unite with Him and live with God forever.
   c. The fulfillment of all the promises of God belonging to God's full rest, a complete satisfaction of the soul.

B. The Sabbath is a symbol of our communion with God.

1. a. Since the Sabbath is a symbol of rest from

sinning, only born-again persons are eager to observe it and enjoy it.

    b.   It is a foretaste, a type, of the life we will enjoy on the new earth when the children of God will enjoy the Sabbath forever. Isaiah 66:22, 23.

2.   In the highest sense, the Sabbath rest symbolizes perfect freedom and rest from sinning, perfect harmony of the soul with God, with oneself, and with one's fellowmen. The Sabbath is a prophecy of a new earth and a new people.

3.   The Sabbath of the Lord is a seal and a sign of His creative and redemptive power. Jesus, as the Creator, rested on the Sabbath day after creation, and as Redeemer after He finished the work of redemption.

4.   The Sabbath is the essence of our communion with God because it provides the ideal physical and spiritual circumstances in which we may commune with Him.

C. The Sabbath is a test of loyalty to God.

Few of either Jews or Gentiles have observed the Sabbath day rest as God commanded. Throughout the ages only a small minority have remained faithful to God's commandments.

1.   Because of their unfaithfulness to this commandment, the Jews were sent by God into Babylonian captivity for seventy years, so that their land might have its Sabbath rest which had been denied to it. Leviticus 26:33-35, 43; 2 Chronicles 36:21.

2.   The Sabbath is still a test of loyalty and love. John 14:15.

If we really love the Lord Jesus Christ, we should from the heart obey faithfully His commandments, including the weekly Sabbath. If we thus unite our hearts with Him in love, we shall enter into His eternal rest. Isaiah 26:2, 3. "So there must still be a promised Sabbath of rest for God's people." Hebrews 4:9, Goodspeed.

Ancient and Modern Controversies Over the Sabbath

INTRODUCTION

The battle between Biblical truth and human error is still raging in the Christian church. Many sincere men are shocked at the errors Satan has succeeded in bringing into the teachings of Christian churches. As in Old Testament times, Satan continues to be successful in shaking, damaging, and destroying the beliefs and faith of men. "The world knew Him not." "His own received Him not." John 1:10, 11. "When the Son of man cometh, shall He find faith on the earth?" Luke 18:8.

I. ISRAEL FAILED TO KEEP THE SABBATH

The keeping of the Sabbath day on Saturday rather than on Sunday is usually considered a genuine Jewish institution. Upon closer study of Israel's attitude toward the Sabbath we find that the nation as a whole did not always observe this holy day in the right spirit.

A. Israel did not keep the Sabbath in Egypt.

During the long centuries of Egyptian bondage the Israelites lost the knowledge of God's law; they disregarded the sacredness of the Sabbath and worked on that day. When Moses was sent by God to deliver His people from slavery, he requested of Pharaoh that the people be allowed to worship God in the proper manner; this included the Sabbath rest. See Pharaoh's complaint, "Ye make them rest from their burdens." Exodus 5:5. When they ceased from working on that day, Pharaoh was displeased and accused them of being idle. The task-masters were instructed to force them to labor on the Sabbath day; to effect this they were required to find their own straw and still produce the same number of bricks each week.

During their wilderness wanderings the Israelites were reminded each week by God of the appointed day of rest and worship; on the seventh day manna was withheld from them, since God had given them a double portion of it on Friday. Nevertheless the people accepted God's commandment very reluctantly. "How long refuse ye to keep My commandments?" Exodus 16:28.

B. **Israel desecrated the Sabbath in Canaan.**

When they were living in Canaan during the time of the judges, and later during the monarchies, Israel and Judah did not consistently observe the Sabbath. They worshiped heathen gods, such as Baal, Moloch, and Ashtoreth. Their idolatry and Sabbath desecration were the chief reasons for their being punished with the Assyrian and Babylonian captivities. Jeremiah 17:21, 27. National ruin was the result of Sabbath breaking.

C. **The Jews at the time of Jesus kept the Sabbath legalistically.**

Because Sabbath desecration was one of the chief reasons for the Babylonian captivity, the men who led the exiles back to Jerusalem—Ezra, Joshua, and their successors—were determined to safeguard the Sabbath institution for posterity. So the people fell into the other extreme. They passed more and more rules and regulations on how to observe the day properly. The Mishna (Jewish code of traditional laws) lists thirty-nine major types of work that were prohibited on the Sabbath. The effect of these human laws was most damaging. And the Talmud elaborated on these hundreds of times. For example, an egg that had been laid on the Sabbath was not to be eaten; no one was allowed to look into a mirror or light a candle on the Sabbath. The Pharisees destroyed the spirit of the law of God by straining out a gnat while figuratively swallowing a camel. They made the Lord's day a burden rather than a delight for the people. By doing this they misrepresented the character of God, making Him appear like a tyrant. It seemed to the people that the Sabbath was more important to God than man himself. This is why Jesus Christ protested: "The Sabbath was made for man, and not man for the Sabbath." Mark 2:27.

II. THE SON OF GOD IS OUR CREATOR AND THE LORD OF THE SABBATH

A. Why Jesus is Lord of the Sabbath.

Jesus Christ is the Creator of the universe (John 1:1-3), Lord of the Sabbath (Mark 2:28), and the Lawgiver on Mount Sinai. Jesus Christ kept His own commandments while on earth. This included Sabbath observance. Genesis 2:1-3; Luke 4:16. When Jesus saw the formal, legalistic way in which men kept the Sabbath, depriving it of its true significance and purpose, He determined to liberate it from human tradition and burdening ceremonies.

B. How did Jesus relate to the Sabbath?

Jesus intentionally brought about several crises on the issue of Sabbath observance. The action He used to restore the Sabbath to its original meaning brought Him into opposition with the rabbis and scribes; it even endangered His life.

1. Jesus healed a man on the Sabbath who had been ill for thirty-eight years. John 5:9, 16. "My Father is working still [by giving rain, sunshine, et cetera], and I am working [by healing the sick]." John 5:17, RSV.
2. His disciples plucked the ears of grain on the Sabbath. Mark 2:23, 24. Jesus defended their action by using the example of David. Mark 2:25, 26. Then

He laid down broad principles. "The Sabbath was made for man . . . : therefore the Son of man is Lord also of the Sabbath." Mark 2:27, 28.

3. Religionists tried to find fault with His teachings. Mark 3:1, 2. They wondered how He would answer their difficult questions. Jesus came right to the point and asked them: "Is it lawful to do good on the Sabbath days?" Mark 3:4.

4. In Jerusalem He healed a woman on the Sabbath who had been crippled for eighteen years. Luke 13:10-13. The ruler of the synagogue reproved Him before the people, but Jesus silenced him effectively while the people rejoiced. Luke 13:14-17.

5. Again the Pharisees attempted to prove Jesus to be a lawbreaker. Jesus unveiled their hypocrisy by asking: "Is it lawful to heal on the Sabbath day?" Luke 14:3. Then He proceeded to heal a sick man and to teach them the principles on which He worked.

C. **Jesus came to magnify the Sabbath, not to abolish it.**

It is evident from these examples that Jesus deliberately desired these crises to occur, even at the risk of death and of alienating the Jewish leaders. Why? Not to change and abolish the Sabbath which He Himself had instituted at creation, but to relieve it from many false concepts and interpretations, to free it from man-made restrictions and traditions that had made this day a burden rather than a delight. He desired to show the real purpose of Sabbath observance, and He sanctified it in the spirit of love and holiness. He could easily have avoided these incidents, but it seemed important to Him that people understand what He had meant by sanctifying the Sabbath.

The question arises: If Jesus intended to change the Sabbath later on by shifting its observance to Sunday, or any other day, or to do away with it altogether as some contend, then why did He make such an effort to teach the correct interpretation of the observance of His commandment? The answer is obvious: Christ did not intend to make any changes in this divine ordinance. Matthew 5:17.

III. SABBATH CONTROVERSIES CONTINUE TO OUR DAY
A. The main point at issue now concerns which day is the Sabbath.

After many centuries the problem of an incorrect interpretation of the fourth commandment is still with us. Every conscientious Christian is eager to do the will of God. The majority of Christians have not been celebrating the seventh day as the Sabbath, but the first.

B. Sabbath observance is as important today as when Christ lived on earth.

Many think that this commandment is of no importance. Maybe they also cannot understand why God considered the eating of the forbidden tree by Adam and Eve of such great import. These people make a serious mistake. Sabbath observance is a solemn commandment of God, confirmed by Jesus Christ. It is a sign of allegiance to Him, an acknowledgment that He is our Creator. When we choose to disregard the Sabbath, we belittle God and deliberately disobey His express command.

IV. THE AUTHORITY OF JESUS CHRIST IS AT STAKE
A. The controversy continues over the Sabbath.

Since Sabbath observance was forbidden by the Laodicean Council, about 360 A.D., this commandment of God has been divorced from the teachings of Jesus Christ. The controversy on this issue continues as in the time of Christ when His life was jeopardized for trying to correct certain false interpretations. In His time He opposed men's laws and traditions because He knew that such laws would result in a mechanical and indifferent observance of His holy day rather than in a closer fellowship with the Creator.

B. **Sabbath observance becomes a test of obedience at the end.**

The Jews opposed Jesus strongly over the question of Sabbath observance. They could not see that He desired to restore this day to its original beauty, to be a blessing and delight for all men.

Some may think that it was a strange thing for Jesus to contend with the religious leaders of His time over such a small issue; yet if Christ were to come to this earth today, as He did 2,000 years ago, He would have to correct the Christian church, since many are not keeping this commandment the way they should. For one thing, many have been keeping the wrong day. Furthermore many are not setting the day apart for communion with Him; rather they spend it recklessly in the pursuit of pleasure. Thereby many have nullified His commandment.

Sabbath observance will become the most controversial issue as we approach the end. God will allow this to happen. He wants to test our faith and obedience. He wishes to ascertain whether a Christian is eager to do His will or would rather follow the traditions of men. A decision is required by all men.

Remember the words of Jesus: "Think not that I am come to destroy the law, or the prophets: I am not come to destroy, but to fulfill." Matthew 5:17. "If ye keep My commandments, ye shall abide in My love; even as I have kept My Father's commandments, and abide in His love." John 15:10.

Why Does Christendom Keep Sunday?

INTRODUCTION

Why does Christendom celebrate Sunday? Why do most Christians worship God on the first day of the week? The answer is that for centuries Christians have been taught to honor this day as a day of rest and worship. Sincere Christians through the centuries desired to obey and honor God in this manner; they were convinced that this was God's holy day. On the other hand, there is a minority of Christians who maintain that the seventh day of the week is the Lord's day. It is called the Sabbath.

Whether to observe God's Sabbath or man's Sunday is a controversial issue. We need the grace of God and His wisdom to help us deal with this problem. We must be careful to avoid emotionalism and prejudice. This issue involves every human being; we must guide men to the Holy Scriptures, the final authority on all matters of faith.

We must not condemn one another but prayerfully seek the truth in the light of the Holy Spirit. This issue is not to be regarded as a rivalry between men; it is a matter between God and man. Let us investigate the origin of Sunday observance, in the spirit of kindness.

I. A TRANSITION IS MADE FROM SABBATH TO SUNDAY

A. The Lord Jesus and the apostles did not change the Sabbath.

1. Jesus Christ instituted the Sabbath at the end of

creation week. He is the Creator. John 1:1-3; Genesis 2:2, 3. He gave the Ten Commandments to Moses on two tables of stone. Exodus 24:12. But they had been known by man since creation and passed on from generation to generation by word of mouth. These commandments were repeated on Mount Sinai and later confirmed by Jesus Christ. Jesus honored His own law and kept it. John 15:10. After finishing the work of redemption He rested on the Sabbath day in the grave. Luke 23:54-56.

2. The apostles made no changes in the law. Romans 3:28, 31; 1 John 5:2, 3; Revelation 22:14; James 2:10.

3. Christians of the first century observed the Sabbath on the seventh day of the week. Paul obeyed this commandment and taught it in Corinth. Acts 18:4, 11. Jesus indicated that the Sabbath would be observed by Christians after His resurrection and ascension when He spoke of the destruction of Jerusalem in A.D. 70. Matthew 24:20.

B. **The emergence of Sunday observance begins in the early centuries.**

The transition from Sabbath to Sunday observance took place gradually over a period of three or four hundred years. The Epistle of Barnabas, and Justin Martyr's First Apology, written about A.D. 150, refer for the first time to the observance of Sunday by Christians. At the close of the second century, Clement of Alexandria and the apocryphal "Gospel According to Peter" mention Sunday as the Lord's day.

During the Jewish revolution, A.D. 132-135, under the leadership of Bar Cocheba, Christians were in an awkward position. Many regarded them as a Jewish sect. When persecution against the Jews broke out, Christian leaders wanted to make a clear differentiation between Judaism and Christianity. Those who kept the Sabbath day were called "Judaizers"; in certain areas they were discouraged from observing this day any longer. Christians were to keep Sunday instead.

The churches in Rome and Alexandria were known for their early transition from Sabbath to Sunday. Alexandria was the seat of Gnosticism. The churches in Jerusalem and Antioch opposed them on this issue. For several centuries great numbers of Christians observed both the Sabbath and Sunday. In the beginning of the third century Tertullian remarked that Jesus Christ had not rescinded the Sabbath.

In the beginning of the fourth century Sunday keeping became more popular. Eusebius, in his Commentary on Psalm 92, wrote: "All things whatsoever it was the duty to do on the Sabbath we have transferred to the Lord's day, since this day is more honorable than the Jewish Sabbath."

C. **Official confirmation given for Sunday.**
1. The Council of Elvira, in A.D. 305, resolved as follows: "If anyone in the city neglects to come to church for three Lord's days, let him be caused to stay away for a short time, so that he may be corrected."—Charles J. Hefele, *History of the Christian Councils,* p. 145, canon 21.
2. On March 7, A.D. 321, Emperor Constantine issued a decree by which he made Sunday a day of worship for all his subjects. "On the venerable Day of the Sun let the magistrates and people residing in cities rest, and let all workshops be closed."
3. About A.D. 360 the Council of Laodicea adopted a canon officially changing the Sabbath to Sunday: "Christians shall not Judaize and be idle on the Sabbath, but shall work on that day; but the Lord's day they shall especially honor, and, as being Christians, shall, if possible, do no work on that day. If, however, they are found Judaizing, they shall be shut out from Christ."—Charles J. Hefele, *History of the Church Councils,* Vol. 2, p. 316.

D. **The Lord's day is the seventh day.**

Some interpreters point to Revelation 1:10 to prove that Sunday is the Lord's day. Others explain that this refers to the "great day of the Lord" as found in Joel 2:11, 31, and Zephaniah 1:14. The only way to decide this matter is by allowing Holy Scripture to explain itself. The Scriptures refer to the seventh-day Sabbath as the Lord's day. Genesis 2:3; Isaiah 58:13; Mark 2:28.

E. **Is Sunday observance a divine memorial to the resurrection of Jesus?**

Many sincere Christians believe that Sunday is a divinely ordained memorial to the resurrection of Jesus Christ. This is not true. The motives are good, but the facts are wrong. If it were left to us to choose a day of worship outside the Sabbath we would prefer to select Friday; for, after all, it is on this day Christ died to redeem mankind. However, we are not asked to choose a day of our own. Jesus decided this matter for us. Just before His death Jesus established a memorial of His death to be observed by all Christians: the Lord's Supper, which reminds us of His atoning death. In the same manner He established another memorial, baptism, which points to His death and *resurrection.* Romans 6:3-5. He did not ask us to establish a further memorial to His resurrection by shifting the Sabbath to Sunday. The Sabbath is a memorial of His act of creation. Exodus 20:8-11.

II. **WHAT DIFFERENCE DOES IT MAKE WHETHER WE OBSERVE THE SEVENTH OR THE FIRST DAY OF THE WEEK?**

A. **What is the significance of observing a day as Sabbath?**

1. Jesus Christ, our Creator, instituted the universal Sabbath day to be observed on the seventh day of the week. He commanded that every man work for six days, then worship Him and rest from his labors on the seventh day. Exodus 20:8-11.

1	2	3	4	5	6	7

If we decide to do the opposite, namely, first rest for a day and then work six days, we honor another lord, the one who is responsible for this substitution.

1	2	3	4	5	6	7

2. There are actually two lords contending for our allegiance. Both have passed laws; these are opposed to one another, and by our decision we select the lord we prefer to obey.

3. If we keep the seventh-day Sabbath, we declare that we accept this day as the sign of our allegiance to our Creator and Redeemer. Exodus 31:16, 17. This passage refers to spiritual Israel. Romans 2:28, 29. On the other hand, if we decide to observe the first day of the week, we indicate that we prefer to give our allegiance to the power that established the observance of this day.

The book of Revelation speaks of the sealing of those who keep the commandments of God and have the testimony of Jesus Christ. Revelation 7:3; 12:17; 14:12. At the same time, it warns us not to accept the sign of allegiance of the other power. The fact is, our choice of the day of worship determines to which lawmaker we are being loyal. Which of these two lords are you worshiping and obeying? That is the question.

B. **Why is this issue important today?**

1. Every age has had a revelation from God of a certain basic truth. 2 Peter 1:12. Noah's message was concerned with moral corruption and the impending

judgment, the Flood. Elijah warned Israel of the worship of Baal, and his message turned the people back to Jehovah. John the Baptist preached the necessity of a genuine conversion experience. Luther emphasized the teaching of salvation by faith. The Baptists taught the world the importance of adult baptism by immersion. Wesley urged mankind to accept the righteousness of Christ. The Sabbath-Sunday controversy was not an issue at any early time. It was to become a dominant issue only at the time of the end of the world. Isaiah 58:12, 13; Revelation 14:6, 12.

2. God will not condemn Christians who have kept Sunday in good faith. If they lacked knowledge of the facts regarding the authentic Lord's day, God will take that into consideration. We are only responsible for the light which we have received or could have received if we had desired it. Luke 12:47, 48; Romans 2:12; Acts 17:30. In past generations many Christians worshiped the Lord on Sunday, and did so in good faith; even today there are many people in every Christian denomination who think Sunday is the Lord's day. God accepts their worship since it stems from a sincere motive.

Not only is it important which day we observe, but also how we observe it. Keeping the right day has little significance if the day is spent apart from God. From that standpoint many Christians observe Sunday more as a day of selfish pleasure than as a day dedicated to reverent communion with Jesus Christ.

C. **This is the last act in the drama of history.**

The time will soon come when the laws of men will be preferred over the laws of God. Laws enforcing the observance of Sunday will be passed, and the issue will be clearly seen by all. A great deal of publicity will accompany these events, so that the whole world will become aware of the Sabbath-Sunday controversy. See Revelation 12:17. Everyone will have to take sides either with God or with Satan.

The institution of the Sabbath was Christ's first act after creation; the enforcement of Sunday as the official day of rest, in place of God's holy day, will be the last act in the drama of the ages. It will occur shortly before the end of the time of probation.

God has a controversy with humanity. "Babylon is fallen, is fallen, that great city, because she made all nations drink of the wine of the wrath of her fornication." Revelation 14:8.

Great principles of loyalty and integrity are at stake in this controversy, principles upon which depends the destiny of our souls.

III. A GREAT DECISION WITH ETERNAL CONSEQUENCES REQUIRES PRAYERFUL CONSIDERATION

A. The gravity of the question involved demands our attention.

When we believe with all our heart in a religious doctrine or in a commandment, we must make sure that it is based on the Bible. We can be sincere and devoted to God and still make serious errors of interpretation. Take Israel as an example. Her people thought they were serving God, but they never accepted His Son as the Messiah.

Most Sunday observers wish truly to serve God. Now that we have called attention to the misinterpretation of the Sabbath, we urge you to test your belief on this point by studying the Holy Scriptures. If you come to the conclusion that the seventh-day Sabbath is the Lord's day, do not hesitate to worship God on this day. Do not reject God's light on this commandment. Jesus said: "Ye made the commandment of God of none effect by your tradition." "But in vain they do worship Me, teaching for doctrines the commandments of men." Matthew 15:6, 9.

Jesus said: "Every plant, which My heavenly Father hath not planted, shall be rooted up." Matthew 15:13. Sunday observance is not a tree planted by the Lord in His garden. This commandment of man will soon be rooted up by the Lord, while Sabbath observance will last throughout eternity. Isaiah 66:22, 23. When Jesus comes, many will say to Him: "Lord, I have done your will and pleasure," but Jesus will answer: "Why call ye Me, Lord, Lord, and do not the things which I say?" Luke 6:46.

B. **The love for Jesus Christ constrains us to do His will, whatever the cost.**

It is not easy to change our minds on an important matter such as this, especially if we have held it sacred since childhood. It is difficult to change our thinking on a teaching that has permeated Christianity for over 1,500 years.

It is hard for Christians to change their day of worship and accept the Sabbath, which is generally considered to be an exclusively Jewish institution, a day which is supposed to have been abolished on the cross and supposedly has no connection with Jesus Christ.

Great hardships are to be expected by the obedient follower of Christ. Sabbath keeping may bring financial difficulties, loss of position, the anger of men, unpopularity, social inconveniences, even difficulties in marriage relations. And yet, God has ordained it. He knew in advance of the trials and difficulties confronting the Christian. Jesus is testing our faithfulness and obedience to His will. A long time ago He tested the faithfulness and obedience of man in the Garden of Eden. He asked man not to touch the forbidden fruit. Today the same test applies to the followers of Christ. He asks us not to work on His holy day but to spend it in intimate fellowship with Him. It is His day.

C. **Sabbath keeping does not save us, but the conscious breaking of it means loss.**

Keeping the Sabbath day holy does not earn salvation for us. We receive salvation by faith and by the grace of God. But if we refuse to obey God's express commandment after receiving enlightenment on this subject, we are in danger of losing eternal life. The test of our faith and love for God is obedience. James 2:17-22; Luke 17:10.

Make certain that you are following the Lord Jesus Christ and obey Him explicitly in all matters. "The world passeth away, and the lust thereof; but he that doeth the will of God abideth forever." 1 John 2:17.

Man Can Obtain Immortality Only Through Jesus Christ

INTRODUCTION

God has endowed man and all other intelligent beings in the universe with a free will, the power of choice. God was aware of the far-reaching implications of such a gift, since it enables anyone to reject Him and His laws, even to organize a rebellion against His government either in heaven or on earth.

I. **SATAN'S REBELLION BECAME A TEST FOR ALL LIVING BEINGS TO REVEAL THEIR LOYALTY TO GOD**
   A. **The heavenly phase of the rebellion.**
      1. From the Bible we learn that Satan tempted the inhabitants of heaven. The majority remained loyal to God, but some rebelled. Revelation 12:4.
      2. The angels of heaven were told by Satan that God was a tyrant; Satan portrayed himself as their true benefactor. Two thirds of the angels remained faithful to God. One third of them, however, sided with Lucifer and rebelled with him against the government of God. They were evicted from heaven and were doomed to live on this planet as demons; they will be destroyed in what the Bible calls "the second death," or hell, after the millennium. Matthew 25:41; Revelation 20:7, 8.
   B. **The earthly phase.**
      1. The men who were living on this earth were also

encouraged by Satan to rebel against God. Satan tempted man to rebel. Man joined Satan in his rebellion and as a result his nature became like Satan's. Man became subject to Satan's rule and a partaker of the second death; man did not possess immortality at any time.

2. Through the wonderful plan of redemption, which God the Father offers to all men through Jesus Christ, every soul has the possibility of choosing, on an individual basis, between eternal life and eternal death. Romans 6:23; Deuternomony 30:19; Revelation 20:14, 15.

II. MAN IS PROMISED IMMORTALITY CONDITIONALLY

A. God alone is immortal. 1 Timothy 6:16.

1. We can only seek after immortality and eternal life. Romans 2:7.

2. Jesus came into this world of sin and death in order to bring us light, hope, life, and immortality. 2 Timothy 1:10.

3. God promises immortality to us under certain conditions. John 3:16; Revelation 22:14.

B. Eternal reward or punishment is without appeal.

Immortality will be bestowed on the children of God at the end of God's overall plan of redemption. It will be bestowed on His followers at His second coming. "Justified, . . . glorified." See Romans 8:29, 30.

1. Immortality is a gift of God. Romans 5:21; 6:23.

2. How will this great change in us take place? Paul, in 1 Corinthians 15:51-54, explains that the mortal will become immortal—corruptible human bodies incorruptible. When Jesus returns, He will resurrect the just who have died and change the bodies of the living righteous. This is the first resurrection, and all who take part in it will receive eternal life. Revelation 20:6; 1 Thessalonians 4:16, 17.

3. At the end of the millennium (1,000 years), the

unrighteous dead will be resurrected. This is the second resurrection. They will be told the reason for their condemnation. They will be doomed to destruction in the lake of fire. It will be seen that every man chose eternal death by his own free will.

4. If the soul of man was immortal, God Himself could not destroy it. The Bible, however, speaks of the total destruction of the unrighteous in a fire that cannot be extinguished. It is called an "eternal fire." The expression "eternal fire" can best be understood in the light of Jude 7. Sodom and Gomorrah are not burning now. Both cities have been totally obliterated. Contrary to the popular opinion of hell, the unrighteous will not burn forever, but will be quickly destroyed through fire. The fire is eternal in the sense that sin and sinners will be eternally destroyed. Sin will not arise a second time. Satan will be destroyed in this fashion. Ezekiel 28:18, 19. Satan (the root) and the unrighteous (the branches) are consigned to destruction. Malachi 4:1, 3.

III. HOW WAS THE FALSE TEACHING OF THE IMMORTALITY OF THE SOUL DEVELOPED, AND WHAT DOES THE BIBLE TEACH ON THIS SUBJECT?

A. Satan is the originator of the teaching regarding the immortality of the soul.

The belief in the immortality of the soul of man originated in paganism. God said: "Thou shalt surely die." Genesis 2:17. Satan, on the other hand, said: "Ye shall not surely die." Genesis 3:4. This is the first record of a lie. John 8:44.

B. Death is sleep.

1. Jesus Christ called the "first death" a sleep. John 11:11-14. Jesus resurrected Lazarus, who had been dead for four days; He called him forth from the tomb, not down from heaven. "Lazarus, come forth." John 11:43.

2. Jesus was for three days in the tomb and not in heaven. John 20:17.
3. The apostle Paul did not expect eternal life to begin after his execution but only on the day of the return of the Lord Jesus. 2 Timothy 4:7, 8. All the other martyrs also have to wait for their resurrection until Jesus returns. Hebrews 11:37-40.

C. **What is the relation between the expressions "the soul" and "the breath of life"?**
1. Jesus formed Adam's body from the earth. Genesis 2:7.
2. God then breathed the breath of life into the finished, but lifeless form, of Adam and he *became* a *living soul.* Before God breathed into him Adam had been a lifeless soul. Genesis 2:7; Job 33:4.
3. The breath of life is God's life-giving energy in man and animal. Genesis 7:21, 22. Bible translators sometimes used the word "soul" or "spirit" in place of "breath of life" and have caused misunderstandings on this subject.

D. **What happens to man after death?**
1. Man is under the curse of sin and death. He does not have a separate undying soul. He returns to dust at death. Genesis 3:19. "The soul that sinneth, it shall die." Ezekiel 18:4.
2. The breath of life itself comes from God. At the moment of death it returns to God. Ecclesiastes 12:7.
3. The process of death in man and animal is the same. At death their breath of life returns to God. Ecclesiastes 3:19-21.
4. The dead do not know or feel anything. Ecclesiastes 9:5, 6, 10; Psalm 146:4.
5. The dead do not praise God anymore. Psalm 115:17; Isaiah 57:1, 2.
6. The dead are not resurrected from their sleep until Jesus returns. Job 14:10-13; John 5:28, 29.

IV. WHAT IS SPIRITUALISM?

A. Satan works miracles to deceive the whole world.

1. Satan and his demons have the ability to impersonate men who have died. Revelation 16:13, 14; 1 Chronicles 10:13. The teaching of the immortality of the soul is the cornerstone of spiritualism. The Bible states that man is mortal; therefore he cannot reappear and communicate with the living. The teaching of the immortality of the soul is one of Satan's master deceptions by which millions are led astray.

2. God has clearly stated that He prohibits man's attempt to contact the dead. Deuteronomy 18:10-12. The man who practices spiritualism becomes the captive of Satan. Jesus, while on earth, was frequently approached by men under the control of demons; He freed them from demon possession.

3. The most masterful deception by Satan will occur when he attempts to impersonate Jesus Christ. This will happen shortly before the return of Jesus. 2 Corinthians 11:13-15. Satan's deception will be so successful that the whole world will worship the false christ—except those who have a living relationship with the true Christ. Revelation 13:8.

B. Followers of Christ will receive immortality at the resurrection.

All the genuine followers of Jesus will receive immortality at Christ's second coming in glory; this is called the "first resurrection." Matthew 16:27. The "second resurrection," involving the unrighteous only, will take place 1,000 years after the "first resurrection." Every man who has died will take part in one of these two resurrections. The question is, in which of these two resurrections will we take part?

Give yourself entirely to Jesus Christ; abide in Him moment by moment. Await His glorious return with joy and expectancy, for He will bring with Him the gift of immortality for all who love and obey Him.

Who Are the Seventh-day Adventists and What Do They Believe?

INTRODUCTION

A minister of a Protestant denomination said this to an Adventist after a prolonged discussion of the teachings of the Seventh-day Adventist Church: "After having analyzed your beliefs concerning Jesus Christ and His gospel, I have come to the conclusion that you are the most misunderstood denomination in Protestantism today."

I. MISTAKEN SOURCES OF INFORMATION

A. Do you have accurate information about Adventists?

Sincere Christian ministers and laymen have made statements regarding Seventh-day Adventists that are incorrect when viewed in the light of what the denomination really believes. Adventists have been classified among the cults, and many do not regard them as Christians. Those who pass judgment on the Adventists have not always studied firsthand information from authentic Adventist books. They have rather consulted opponents of the Adventist message. In order to be able to make an objective judgment of this denomination, a person should communicate with competent Adventist spokesmen and study Adventist books that have been approved by the official denominational authorities.

An inquirer in the time of Jesus who went to the Pharisees and Sadducees to find out what Jesus taught

(129)

would have received misleading information from these sources. He would not have learned from them what Jesus Christ stood for. The same principle is true today.

B. **Why are Adventists called "unchristian"?**

There are reasons why certain religious authorities claim that Adventists do not believe in the deity of Jesus Christ, His preexistence, His equality with God the Father, His finished work of atonement on the cross, et cetera.

1. Many of the founders of the Adventist church were Trinitarians; they believed in all the fundamentals of the gospel of Jesus Christ. Others who were helping develop this new church had been members of religious movements that were militantly Arian and anti-Trinitarian. They denied the divinity of Jesus Christ. In those early days these men were allowed to publish books and articles for the Seventh-day Adventist Church. There were no official reading committees as yet to examine these publications before they were published in the printing plants of the church. In the formative years of the church there was no tightly knit organization that could prevent such literature from being distributed through the church.

2. This made it possible for individuals to publish their personal views of doctrine in Adventist publications. For all practical purposes it looked like their views represented the whole church. This was not the case. The majority of the leaders did not endorse these unscriptural views. Inquirers into the Adventist position should avail themselves of those books and magazines that have been officially approved.

3. Although the church has made efforts to withdraw all books and magazines that contain these personal views of Adventists which do not agree with the official position of the church, critics have been successful in obtaining enough copies of this false

material to misrepresent the theological position of the church. These critics feel that they are fully justified in referring to these writings.

C. **Theologians have changed their views of Adventism.**

A few years ago the late Dr. Donald R. Barnhouse, editor of *Eternity* magazine, contacted the world headquarters of the Seventh-day Adventists asking for material he desired to use for his new book on religious cults. After he studied the theology of the Seventh-day Adventist Church for two years, during which time he had numerous meetings with the leaders of this church, he discovered that his views of Adventism had been wrong. He revised his thinking, based on the new facts he received, and published his findings in several articles. He called Adventists "brethren in Christ." This is not an isolated instance. Sincere men and women who had been misled by erroneous information have corrected their views after receiving the facts.

II. WHAT ARE THE OBJECTIVES OF THE ADVENTIST CHURCH?

A. **Adventists have a message for the world.**

1. The Adventist Church is a movement born out of Bible prophecy. In Revelation 14:6-12, God points to a movement symbolized by three angels carrying a distinct message to all mankind. The Adventist Church is the fulfillment of this prophecy. This does not mean that genuine Christians are to be found only among Seventh-day Adventists.

2. Members of the Adventist Church have specific goals.

    a. To proclaim the faith of Jesus Christ as it was taught in the first century A.D. Revelation 14:6.

    b. To warn all men of God's judgment and urge them to accept God's mercy. Matthew 24:14; Revelation 14:7.

        c. To prepare a people for the glorious appearing of Jesus Christ at His second coming. Revelation 14:12.

B. Adventists believe there are only two ways of life.

    1. The two ways are pointed out by the Bible.

        a. One is the way of holiness and eternal life. Isaiah 35:8; Proverbs 15:24.

        b. The other is the way of sin and death. Psalm 139:24; Matthew 7:13.

    2. From God's point of view there are not thirteen world religions and 280 denominations, but only two classes of people; namely,

        a. Those who love Jesus Christ, obey Him, and seek to enter His kingdom.

        b. Those who do not love Him, do not wish to obey Him, and do not seek His kingdom.

III. SUMMARY OF THE BELIEFS OF THE ADVENTIST CHURCH

Adventists do not claim a creed, but rather consider the whole Bible as the basis of their beliefs. They do not feel that a man-made creed adequately expresses the teachings of a denomination. In order to show what Adventists believe, it is necessary to give a lengthy description of their doctrinal position. Recently this was compiled by Dr. LeRoy Froom, Professor Emeritus of Historical Theology of Andrews University.

    A. The first group of basic doctrines—shared with all evangelical Protestants.

        1. The true and living God, our heavenly Father, the First Person of the Godhead, is revealed in the Old and New Testaments as the Sovereign Maker, Upholder, and Ruler of the universe, and is eternal, omnipotent, omniscient, and omnipresent.

        2. The Godhead—the three Persons of the heavenly Trio, or Trinity—is comprised of Father, Son, and Holy Spirit.

3. The Holy Scriptures are the inspired revelation of the will of God, and His way for man, and the Bible is the full, sufficient, and sole rule of faith and practice of the Christian.

4. Jesus Christ, the Second Person of the Godhead, the instrument in the creation and upholding of all things, is God in the highest sense, eternally pre-existent, and coexistent with the Father from all eternity; He was neither created nor derived, His life being original, unborrowed, and underived.

5. The Holy Spirit, the Third Person of the Godhead, is likewise a personal Being, sharing all the divine attributes of both Father and Son. He is Christ's representative on earth, leading sinners to repentance and obedience.

6. The Second Person of the Godhead became incarnate in the Person of Jesus Christ, through miraculous conception and virgin birth, and lived an absolutely sinless life during the period of His incarnation among men. Thus He could die as our sinless Sacrifice and Saviour and is man's Saviour from sin.

7. The vicarious, sacrificial, atoning death of Jesus Christ on the cross, once for all and all-sufficient for the redemption of a lost race, was potentially and provisionally for all, but is actually and experimentally only for those who avail themselves of its provisions.

8. Jesus Christ, after His death and burial, rose literally and bodily from the grave and gave His final instruction for His church to His disciples before His ascension.

9. Jesus Christ ascended literally and bodily into heaven, as foretold in Old Testament prophecy and attested by the New Testament records.

10. Christ our Sacrifice now serves as our ministering High Priest and Mediator before the Father, applying the benefits of the atonement He completed on the

cross, which ministry will culminate in His transcendent work as Judge.

11. Jesus Christ will return in a personal, literal, premillennial second advent, as King of kings and Lord of lords, which coming they believe to be imminent, but without setting any time. They hold His second advent to be the sole hope of a disintegrating world that is hastening on to self-destruction.

12. Man was originally created sinless, but by his subsequent fall he entered into a state of alienation and depravity from which he must be redeemed in order to be saved.

13. Such salvation for man is effected solely through Christ, by grace alone, through faith in His atoning blood—works and obedience following as the inevitable result, not the cause or means, of salvation.

14. Entrance upon the new life in Christ is by regeneration, or the new birth, effected by the creative work of the Holy Spirit.

15. Through faith man is justified, and is delivered from the guilt and penalty of sins that are past.

16. The justified believer is sanctified by the indwelling of Christ through the Holy Spirit, and is thus emancipated from the power and dominion of sin in this present life.

17. The justified and sanctified believer will be glorified at the second coming of Christ, and the attendant resurrection or translation of the saints, and thus be freed forever from the very presence and possibility of sin at our Lord's return.

18. There will be a judgment of all men, with its just and righteous decisions irrevocable for all eternity. They believe that the hour of that judgment has come.

19. The everlasting gospel of the impending kingdom is to be preached as a witness to all the world—this to be followed by the cataclysmic end of the world, or age, at the second advent.

B. **The second category—additional doctrines held in varying forms by conservative Christians.**

1. Man is free to choose or reject the offer of salvation through Christ. Adventists are in the main Arminians, not Calvinistic predestinarians; they do not believe that God has predetermined that some men shall arbitrarily be saved and others lost.

2. The moral law of the Ten Commandments, or Decalogue, is the unchanging standard of life and conduct for men in all ages, or dispensations. They believe that the Decalogue has not been changed or abolished. They are not antinomians.

3. Baptism should be administered to rational and accountable persons by single immersion. They believe it is not rightly administered, Biblically, by sprinkling, pouring, or even triune immersion.

4. At creation man was made a candidate for immortality, and placed on test. They do not believe in universal, natural, innate, indefeasible immortality. They believe in conditional immortality, and eternal life only in and through Christ for the saved.

5. The wicked, in the execution of the irrevocable sentences of the judgment, will, after due punishment, be ultimately and utterly destroyed in the lake of fire. They do not believe in an eternally burning hell in which the wicked will be tormented throughout ages without end. The execution of the judgment will eventuate in a clean universe, forever undefiled by Satan, sin, or sinners.

6. The seventh day of the week is the Sabbath for all men, of all dispensations. They believe that the Sabbath has never been abolished or changed to the first day, that it is not merely a seventh part of time.

7. The principle of tithing is for all men, as God's plan for the support of the ministry of His church in all ages. They believe that tithing was not simply for the Jews.

8. God brought the world into its finished form in six literal days, by fiat creation at creation week. They do not believe that creation was accomplished by a vast evolutionary process, extending over endless ages.

9. The true and correct view of prophetic interpretation is that of the continuous-fulfillment historical school. They do not accept either the Counter-Reformation futurist (gap theory) or Preterist (all past) schools of interpretation. They believe in the premillennialist view of the apostolic church, not in the Catholic Augustinian, or the Protestant Whitbyan postmillennial, or amillennial postulates.

10. Church and state should operate in basically separate spheres. They believe that the church should not dominate the state and that the state should not govern the church in attempting the control of man's conscience or his religious views or activities.

11. The preparatory ordinance of feet washing, at the time of the Lord's Supper, as instituted by Christ Himself, is to be practiced by all Christians. They believe that this rite was not limited to apostolic times and was not designated for mere token performance.

12. They should abstain from alcoholic beverages, tobacco, and narcotics, and Biblically "unclean" foods (such as the flesh of scavengers). They believe that such indulgences are not compatible with the principles and practices enunciated by Christ and the apostles. They believe that our bodies are the temple of the Holy Ghost and that as such should not be defiled.

C. **The third group of basic beliefs.**

This category embraces truths predicted in the Scripture for *last day emphasis,* therefore neither due nor applicable in past generations, now due and imperative and being given their designated emphasis today, in the giving of which Adventists believe they have a definite part.

1. There are two distinct phases to Christ's post-ascension High Priestly ministry in the sanctuary—declared by the Scriptures to be in heaven—the second and final phase of such ministry, in these latter times, being the prophesied judgment phase in which the destinies of all mankind are forever settled *before* Christ returns in power and glory. We are now in that predicted "hour" of God's judgment.

2. The seal of God, and the mark of the "beast," are respectively symbols of contrasting *last day* loyalty either to God and truth, or subservience to apostasy and error, predominant in the great final conflict between the forces of good and evil, climaxing just before Christ comes the second time and probationary time closes forever for all mankind.

3. The symbolic flying "angels" of Revelation 14 represent the cumulative heralding of God's last threefold message to the world, to prepare its inhabitants for the soon returning King of glory, Jesus Christ from heaven.

4. These respective messages announce the hour of God's judgment as now here, warn against the dominance of apostasy in the church at large, and proclaim the dreadful punishment of those who willfully accept the mark of apostasy in the world's last crisis hour, when mankind makes its ultimate choice between revealed right and wrong, truth and error.

5. The spirit of prophecy is one of the abiding gifts of the Spirit, to be specially manifest for guidance and counsel and to draw men back to the all-sufficient Bible platform, in the remnant or final segment of the Christian church of the centuries. This gift has appeared in the witness of the Seventh-day Adventist Church.

CONCLUSION

A. **Adventists consider themselves part of the vast body of born-again Christians.**

Adventists believe that their faith is grounded on the Holy Scriptures, and that they carry a special message for the close of human history. They do not consider themselves to be superior Christians because they have been chosen to proclaim God's closing message. They do not claim that membership in the church saves a man or that every Adventist is a born-again Christian. They are quick to point out that quite a number of Adventists have a superficial knowledge of Jesus Christ, have never surrendered their lives to Him, are not wearing Christ's robe of righteousness, and that before Jesus returns many lukewarm Adventists will apostatize and leave the church. Adventists state that other Christian denominations contain many born-again persons who will be saved.

B. **Sincere Adventists are pursuing three objectives.**

1. The renunciation of self and acceptance of the righteousness of Jesus Christ, to live in constant union with Him through the Holy Spirit.

2. Obedience of the commandments of God and the practice of the principles of Jesus Christ and the love of our fellowman through the indwelling spirit of Christ.

3. Making known to everyone the excellency and glory of our Lord and Saviour Jesus Christ, proclaiming all His teachings and principles, preparing themselves and others for the return of Jesus Christ.

   "Henceforth there is laid up for me the crown of righteousness, which the Lord, the righteous Judge, will award to me on that day, and not only to me but also to all who have loved His appearing." 2 Timothy 4:8, RSV.

   If we want to be saved, we must be among those who love His appearing!

How Can Man Triumph in the Face of Objections and Obstacles?

INTRODUCTION

Whatever venture we undertake, whatever vocation we pursue, there is always a certain risk involved, a price to be paid. The same is true for following Jesus Christ.

Every man who exchanges his loyalty to this world for loyalty to Jesus Christ will find out that Satan becomes his open enemy. Difficulties will arise on every side. This has been the lot of every child of God, but Jesus promises victory to every faithful soul. Jesus Himself was not spared suffering. Hebrews 2:10; 5:8. Believers have to walk the same path that He walked. Acts 14:22.

I. VICTORIES OBTAINED THROUGH CHRIST IN THE LIFE OF EVERY BELIEVER

Ellen G. White, who wrote an inspiring commentary on the Bible, stated in her book, *The Desire of Ages*, page 679: "He knew that truth, armed with the omnipotence of the Holy Spirit, would conquer in the contest with evil. . . . He knew that the life of His trusting disciples would be like His, a series of uninterrupted victories, not seen to be such here, but recognized as such in the greater hereafter. . . .

"Courage, energy, and perseverance they must possess. Though apparent impossibilities obstruct their way, by His grace they are to go forward. Instead of deploring difficulties, they are called upon to surmount them. They are to despair of nothing, and to hope for everything. . . . It is His purpose that the highest

(139)

influence in the universe, emanating from the source of all power, shall be theirs."

A. Christ is always triumphant.

While on earth, Jesus Christ overcame sin and Satan. Every day brought a triumph over the attacks of the adversary. These victories are repeated in the life of every surrendered person. They are made possible through the grace and power of the indwelling Spirit of Christ.

B. Defeats are turned into victories.

Disappointments, difficulties, and suffering are some of our best teachers. Through them we learn lessons which we would otherwise never learn. By faith in Jesus we can turn defeats into victories.

C. Do not look at the obstacles but to Jesus.

When you suffer for the sake of Jesus and are under great pressure because of obstacles put in your way, do not keep your eyes on your antagonists or on your difficulties, but look upon Jesus. He can change the situation unexpectedly in your favor. Do not rely on what your eyes can see, but look on the unseen things wrought by God. 2 Corinthians 4:17, 18.

When Peter stepped out of the boat, he walked with a growing sense of security on the waves because he kept his eyes fixed on Jesus Christ. When he took his eyes off Jesus Christ and looked at the threatening waves around him, he began to sink. Are you doing the same thing Peter did in your difficult situation? Jesus says to all of us, Oh, you of little faith, do not look at the waves around you; never listen to the violent noise of the storm raging around you, but look steadfastly on Me; I am walking on the waves of your difficulties. Endure, "as seeing Him who is invisible"! Hebrews 11:27.

II. MANY SMALL VICTORIES PREPARE THE SOUL FOR THE FINAL VICTORY

A. What is the purpose of obstacles?

1. Difficulties and struggles are the heritage of Christ's

true followers. John 15:18, 19; 2 Corinthians 4:8, 9.

2. Why does God send these trials into our lives? "The trying of your faith worketh patience." James 1:3. "Tribulation worketh patience; and patience, experience; and experience, hope." Romans 5:3, 4. Trials bring about moral and spiritual cleansing. Malachi 3:3.

3. Faith that has been tested is more precious than pure gold. 1 Peter 1:7. "Many shall be purified, and made white, and tried." Daniel 12:10.

B. **How can redeemed men become triumphant and victorious?**

1. Before you agree to follow Jesus Christ, count the cost. Luke 14:28.

2. Put away all hindrances that stand between Christ and you. "Strip off every handicap, strip off sin with its clinging folds." Hebrews 12:1, Moffatt. "Consider Him that endured such contradiction of sinners against Himself." Hebrews 12:3.

3. Never depend on yourself. "Lean not unto thine own understanding." Proverbs 3:5.

4. Look to Jesus and never to men. "Looking unto Jesus." Hebrews 12:2.

5. Jesus predicted that following Him meant suffering. Matthew 5:10-12.

6. Trust in Christ's unfailing promises and help. 2 Corinthians 1:20.

7. Look to the reward. Hebrews 11:26.

8. The power of grace exceeds the power of sin. Romans 5:20.

C. **Victory is a gift of God.**

1. Behold the precious promises of victory: "Thanks be to God, which giveth us the victory through our Lord Jesus Christ." 1 Corinthians 15:57. "In all these things we are more than conquerors through Him that loved us." Romans 8:37. "Wherever I go,

thank God, He makes my life a constant pageant of triumph in Christ." 2 Corinthians 2:14, Moffatt.

2. Victory is ours through faith: "This is the victory that overcometh the world, even our faith." 1 John 5:4. God honors our faith by doing great things for us. Hebrews 11:33, 34. "To him that overcometh will I grant to sit with Me in My throne." Revelation 3:21.

D. Scripture is full of encouraging admonitions.

1. "Commit thy way unto the Lord; . . . and He shall bring it to pass." Psalm 37:5. "Call upon Me in the day of trouble: I will deliver thee, and thou shalt glorify Me." Psalm 50:15. "The Lord delivereth him out of them all." Psalm 34:19. "God is . . . a very present help in trouble." Psalm 46:1. "Let us therefore come boldly unto the throne of grace." Hebrews 4:16. "Casting all your care upon Him." 1 Peter 5:7.

2. We must realize that the life of faith is a continuous fight. 2 Timothy 4:7; 1 Timothy 6:12.

   We must not become frightened when our lives take strange turns. 1 Peter 4:12. We must always be prepared for more severe tests. Jeremiah 12:5.

3. Behold God's precious promise to those who love Him. "We know that all things work together for good to them that love God." Romans 8:28. See also Ephesians 3:20.

E. Take your stand for what you know to be right, even at the cost of becoming unpopular.

1. It is easy to stand up for a popular cause. It is pleasant to enjoy popularity. We must remember, however, that following Jesus Christ and proclaiming His gospel have never been popular; the masses did not hail Him. To be a disciple or a messenger of Christ was never a popular cause. "If any man will come after Me, let him deny himself." Matthew 16:24. Jesus Christ expects the believer to stand up

for Him and His teachings even if no one else supports him. He must be ready to bear the heat of criticism and not cringe when he has been misunderstood or when his adversaries call him by evil names. Only challenged, tested, and victorious Christians will ever enter the gates of heaven.

2. The cause of Jesus Christ, the demonstration and propagation of His gospel, needs men and women of courage and determination in times of crisis such as are coming over the world now. Christ is looking for men and women who cannot be bought at any price but will take their stand firmly for Him and His principles, although the whole world might turn against them.

III. THE GREATEST VICTORY OF ALL IS THE CONQUEST OF SELF

A. Self-discipline is needed.

When we are under pressure of great obstacles, our minds and bodies must be trained and disciplined as are the athletes when preparing for the Olympic games. 1 Corinthians 9:24-27.

Our eternal life is at stake in every test and trial. Jesus expects us to abide in Him and claim His power to succeed in the test. We must be overcomers in His strength.

B. We need the whole armor of God.

Paul urges the believer to put on the whole armor of God and conquer in the name of the Lord Jesus Christ. Ephesians 6:11, 12. No victory is won in our own strength. God accepts our willingness to triumph over all difficulties and empowers us to do so by His grace.

C. The dross in our lives must go.

In God's furnace of trials the dross in our lives is consumed; our character is purified as gold. Remember that the three young Hebrews in the Old Testament story were not saved *from* the furnace but were saved *in* the furnace. The tried and tested faith of a believer is precious in the eyes of Jesus Christ. 1 Peter 1:6, 7.

D. **The victor receives a crown.**

There must have been many who were disappointed when Jesus died on the cross. They must have considered His life a failure. I can hear them say that Jesus was a worthy man, but He lost His battle. Little did they realize that the cross is the greatest victory ever wrought in the history of the whole universe. The followers of Jesus Christ have never been recognized by the world as conquerors; they have never been thought of as having reached the highest goals in life. When believers enter the kingdom of God and are given the crown of victory, the whole universe will shout with acclamation, "Here are those who were lost but received the victory through the Lamb!"